TO THE TOP OF THE MOUNTAIN

By William N. Abeloe

To the Top of the Mountain

St. Leander's, 1864-1964

Historic Spots in California (with Hoover, Rensch and Rensch)

St. Anthony's Yesterday and Today

St. John's Golden Jubilee Album

The Missions of Baja California (educational color filmstrip)

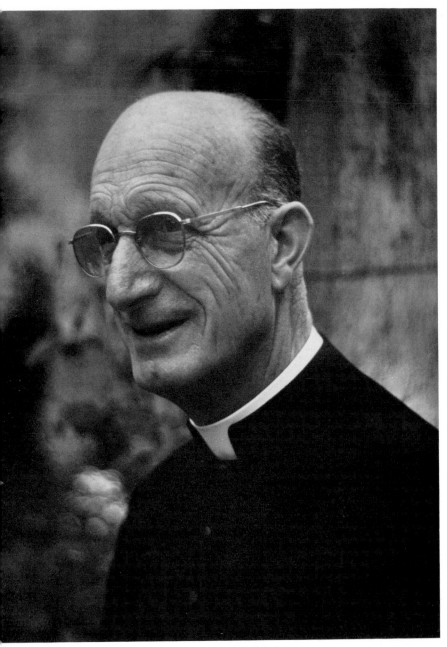

Father Umberto Olivieri
1884-1973
Photographed by author on Ordination Day, June 22, 1958

TO THE TOP
OF THE MOUNTAIN

The Life of Father Umberto Olivieri,
"Padre of the Otomis"

William N. Abeloe

With a Foreword by
His Eminence
MIGUEL DARIO CARDINAL MIRANDA
Archbishop of Mexico City

ILLUSTRATED

Exposition Press   *Hicksville, New York*

NIHIL OBSTAT:
James F. Keane
Censor Librorum

IMPRIMATUR:
†Floyd L. Begin
Bishop of Oakland

October 6, 1975

Any profit that the author might stand to gain from the sale of this book will be sent to the Valley of the Mezquital for the continuation of Father Olivieri's work.

Excerpts from the Holy Bible, Confraternity Edition © used herein by permission of the Confraternity of Christian Doctrine, copyright owner.

Scripture texts used in this work taken from the NEW AMERICAN BIBLE, copyright © 1970 by the Confraternity of Christian Doctrine, Washington, D.C., are used by the permission of said copyright owner. No part of the NEW AMERICAN BIBLE may be reproduced in any form without permission in writing from the Confraternity of Christian Doctrine, Washington, D.C.

FIRST EDITION

© 1976 by William N. Abeloe

Library of Congress Catalog Card Number: 76-7187

ISBN 0-682-48558-6

Printed in the United States of America

For
SISTER JO,
who also climbed
to the top of the mountain

CONTENTS

FOREWORD

"Ah, Papà, you renounced your beautiful home, your family, your place in high society, you even renounced your intellectual life, but you ended by finding everything. Had you remained a great captain, or a great lawyer, or a great professor, you would never have received the homage and the veneration and the devotion manifested today by these simple people as they marched behind you to the cemetery. You have a large family in the United States, an even larger one in Italy, but I am the only one here with any of the old ties. Instead it is the people to whom you gave yourself completely who are with you now."—*Sister Josephine Olivieri Tarquini*

Who could add anything to these most beautiful thoughts? They come from the heart of a daughter consecrated to the service of the needy even before her adoptive father was consecrated a priest to the service of the least and most impoverished people, yet people most beloved by the Father of mercies and the God of all consolation.

For our happiness and the edification of everyone who reads this enchanting book, Father William Abeloe paints through these pages a beautiful mural of the soul and the life of the dearly loved and unforgettable Father Umberto Olivieri. The author leaves out no detail of the figure of this man, so total in his self-giving, who had been his professor at the University of Santa Clara.

But, on the other hand, how can we forget the bond we have with him? We were linked with him by time and work. When we lived in faraway Rome, we were touched by the disaster of Avezzano, in which 58,000 persons perished and which marked for Father Olivieri a new and unknown path in his life. We lived the same anguishes of all those who in one way or another were involved in the terrible World War I, when we were studying in the Colegio Pio Latino Americano in Rome. Who could foresee what would happen years later in the Valley of the Mezquital?

When we were named, by the Will of God, bishop of Tulancingo (1937-1956), our main concern was always our Otomi Indians, with hearts of gold, bright faces, and full of confidence when they felt themselves understood and loved. Lacking all things, they needed what we had to give, and they would have had next to nothing were it not for the great longings of our heart to strike at the very root of the problem and initiate radical solutions that would cover equally the religious, cultural, economic and social aspects of the community. Having found an echo of our pastoral anxieties in the sympathetic heart of Monseñor Luis María Martínez, who was then archbishop of Mexico City, we could put into action, with a decidedly missionary intention, a plan of vast proportions, which would culminate years later in the creation of a new diocese, Tula.

Among the first projects undertaken to give special attention to the Indians of the Mezquital, a call went out to the missionary priests of the Oblates of St. Joseph of Asti, Italy, whom the Apostolic Delegate at that time, Monseñor Guillermo Piani, had known in the Philippines.

If, as we have always thought, our life is a link in a chain in which many have come before us and many others will come after, the most providential arrival of Brother Olivieri was a link of gold in this work for the benefit of the Indians of the Mezquital.

We did everything in our power that His Holiness Pope Pius XII, of happy memory, might deign to grant the necessary dispensations for Brother Olivieri to be ordained a priest. This incident united us to him more closely. Finally, as archbishop of Mexico City, we came in contact with him at the end of the earthly part of his precious life, loaded with the fruits of love. At his deathbed we had the enormous happiness of giving him a final embrace and a *gracias* from the depths of our heart.

Father Olivieri is a link in this chain for the redemption of our Indian brothers. Many before him have offered their lives in that ideal, many others will follow him, inspired by his example, and will be, like him, links of gold that continue to unite us to all who are engaged in the most beautiful work, inspired by God, that can be undertaken by a human being—to consecrate one's life to serve those who are most in need, to love the most forgotten, to give oneself without measure to the most dispossessed.

This book is an eloquent testimony to one life so offered in the noblest of causes.

+ Miguel Darío Cardinal Miranda
ARCHBISHOP PRIMATE OF MEXICO

Mexico, D.F.
April 21, 1976

PREFACE

This book is written as a testimony to the grace of God in the life of one man. May his story bring a message of courage and peace to a troubled Church and a troubled world. May it give a measure of comfort to divorced Catholics who bear a heavy cross. May it inspire older persons to consider spending their leisure years in loving service of God and their fellow-man.

Originally this was to have been an autobiography. Father Olivieri's death necessitated a change of plans. I have tried to tell the story as he might have told it, with frequent quotations from his letters, especially in the later chapters.

Many persons have contributed to whatever value this little book may have. I am deeply grateful to His Eminence Miguel Darío Cardinal Miranda, Archbishop of Mexico City, for his kindness in writing the Foreword.

Sister Josephine Olivieri Tarquini, the beloved "Sister Jo" of St. Vincent's Hospital, Indianapolis, gave help, encouragement and valuable criticism over a period of several years.

Miss Mary Peschges, now of Le Sueur, Minnesota, transcribed many hours of tape recordings and typed the final manuscript.

To them, and to all who have helped by sharing memories or photographs, by financial assistance, or in any other way, sincere and prayerful thanks.

FATHER WILLIAM N. ABELOE
El Cerrito, California
September 12, 1975

TO THE TOP OF THE MOUNTAIN

One

TO THE TOP
OF THE MOUNTAIN

The professor was about to climb the mountain.

"Lonely as God, and white as a winter moon, Mount Shasta starts up sudden and solitary from the heart of the great black forests of Northern California." So wrote Joaquin Miller, the "Poet of the Sierra," who had climbed the majestic peak several times in his youth. The Indians believed that the Great Spirit had made this mountain first of all His creation. Shasta is an extinct volcano. Its summit, 14,162 feet, dominates the landscape for more than a hundred miles. Since the first recorded ascent in 1854, it has become a popular challenge for mountain climbers from all over the world.

Now, here was the professor, ready to join their ranks. It was midsummer 1938, and he was fifty-four. He had always loved the outdoors. His work kept him inside most of the time, and he longed for weekends and vacations when he could get away and immerse himself in the beauty of God's creation. As a young man in his native Italy he had done considerable mountain climbing, but you wouldn't call him an expert by any means. He was staying with friends at McCloud, a small town by the foot of Mount Shasta, and they helped him to outfit for the expedition and to secure the services of a local guide.

You could say that it all started as a dare, although nobody but himself actually dared him to do it. Three Italian-born acquaintances, former competitors of his when he was a banker in San Francisco, had shortly before tried, and failed, to conquer

3

the summit of Mount Shasta. They had really made a production of it. They even chartered a special train to take them and their camp followers to Siskiyou County. The Italian-language newspapers in San Francisco created quite a commotion over them. And then came the moment of truth. The mountain proved too much for them. They had to abandon their extravaganza in mid-ascent and return to San Francisco in defeat.

The professor heard about the fiasco. He laughed. An old Spanish proverb ran through his mind: "They went to shear the sheep and got sheared themselves!" He was especially amused because he had long felt that one of the would-be climbers needed a lesson in humility. This man had married the daughter of the largest stockholder of one of the principal banks and had become senior vice-president of the bank, and the professor had found him unbearable.

Suddenly it came to him. "I can do it! I just HAVE to do it!"

And then the conditioning process began. Every free day for several weeks found him strengthening his legs by climbing on Mount Hamilton, not far from the University of Santa Clara, where he taught romance languages. He had gone there many times before on outings with some of his favorite students. It was not a difficult mountain to climb, slightly better than 4,000 feet above sea level, but it was an excellent place to practice until the day when he would be ready to take on Mount Shasta.

That day had now arrived. The professor laced up his favorite hiking boots and put on a battered felt hat to keep his balding pate warm. That unlovely piece of headgear was his inseparable companion in the mountains, and he wore it as if it were a jeweled tiara. His family used to be ashamed of it, but he would laughingly retort that it was his undeniable proof of Roman nobility. There is a well-known saying that only a Roman prince can wear an old hat with an air of elegance. The guide gathered together the essential tools of mountain climbing, both men strapped packs on their backs, and they were off.

They began the ascent between four and five o'clock in the

morning in order to be able to return by evening. The first part of the climb was relatively easy. The trail was well marked. The birds twittering in the tops of the tall trees and the rising sun playing light-and-shadow games through the leafy branches made for a stimulating, yet relaxing, hike. The two men rested for a few moments in the shade. A butterfly alit on a nearby rock and heaved its multicolored wings back and forth as it, too, rested. The professor contemplated the fragile insect and his face became radiant with joy. "How great must be the beauty of God if He could make such a beautiful creature!" He was considered a deeply religious person, a daily communicant in the Mission Church on the Santa Clara campus. About fifteen years earlier he had begun what was to be a lifelong study of St. Francis of Assisi and his influence upon the world. That great lover of nature had taught the professor to see the hand of God in every work of creation.

As the climbers approached timberline they were treated to another side of God's hand. The deeply fluted slopes of the mountain were covered with snow. Only here and there could they see the porous lava rock which underlay the white blanket. In the distance they spied one of the great glaciers, relic of a late ice age which centuries ago had played its part in sculpturing the old volcanic mountain into its present shape. The professor knew that, drop by drop, the liquefied ice of that glacier would ultimately find its way into the mighty Sacramento River coursing down to San Francisco Bay. It was magnificent!

But now the real work began. The snow had melted in many places yet had left a glittering crust to deceive the eye and entrap the foot. The professor fell again and again but picked himself up to continue the trek. Once he sank so deeply into a drift that his guide had to use both hands to extricate him. A chill wind lashed at his clothing and appeared to be winning the battle it was waging with the sun trying to warm him from above.

Rest stops became more frequent, wherever a ledge provided them room. The professor began to doubt that he could make it. Would an avalanche sweep them into oblivion? Perhaps he had better turn back now, before it was too late. He muttered under his breath that surely the guide had chosen the wrong route. There must be an easier way. How could he have allowed himself to be apprenticed to this man when there were so many better guides available? It was a situation that called for prayer, but he did not remember to pray. The more he thought, the more he was overcome by exhaustion. He took a sip of pineapple juice from the flask in his pack. He had remembered the words of his young, vivacious daughter, now off on a trip to Italy: "Papà, when you feel very tired, you drink some of this pineapple juice, and you will feel better." He forced himself to his feet and trudged on.

Hours later—it seemed to him like days—they came to a hot spring some distance below the summit, a delightful spot to tarry a moment and a reminder that the ancient fires of Mount Shasta were still burning somewhere deep in its interior. The professor was told that it wouldn't be long now, and he pushed on with renewed vigor.

Just a few hundred feet below the crest he was again vanquished by fatigue. He had been climbing for twelve hours. "I can't make it!" he thought to himself. Alternately he glanced at the azure sky and squinted at the snow glinting in the afternoon sun. Then he looked up to the summit where the guide was awaiting him. He remembered the San Francisco bankers. He imagined what the Italian newspapers would say. "I just HAVE to make it!" he shouted aloud.

Summoning all his strength he fairly ran to the top of the mountain. He opened the copper box and wrote his name in the register. He flung out his arms and proclaimed triumphantly to the panorama around and below him: "I MADE IT!"

* * *

The priest studied the steep trail and shook his head sadly.

The Valley of the Mezquital in central Mexico is not a single valley but a large region with several valleys, as well as many mountains and hills, gullies and dry streambeds. It is arid and inhospitable, but it has been the home for many centuries of the Otomi Indians. Vegetation is sparse. Only the maguey, like a cactus but with fleshy leaves, seems to flourish naturally in the Mezquital. It is the source of food, drink, clothing and shelter for the Otomis. The implacable sun scorches the land in summer and then abandons it to freezing winds in winter. Rainfall is rare in either season.

Now it was the heart of winter. One of the Franciscan Sisters of Orizabita, a tiny and isolated settlement in the Mezquital, had come to the larger town of Ixmiquilpan to find the priest. She had been approached by two Indians living up in the mountains beyond Orizabita who came to tell her that an old woman, the mother of one of them, lay dying and was in need of the ministrations of a priest. The distance and the condition of the roads made it impossible for them to transport the sick woman to the hospital in Ixmiquilpan. They agreed, however, to carry her from her hut at the top of a hill down to a spot which would be the farthest point that the sister would be able to reach in her car.

She found the priest at his home and explained the situation. Without a word he reached for the Holy Oils and boarded the car. The two proceeded cautiously, yet with all possible haste, over the rocky tracks to the place where they expected to find the old woman. They found instead only her son and his friend. It seemed that her condition had worsened and she could not be moved. The Indians begged the priest to go to her humble home.

The priest was not prepared for this. He looked at the trail, if it can be called that, going up the mountainside and concluded, "I'll never make it." The men pleaded with him, clarifying beyond doubt that the old mother could not live more than a few hours and that she had long been separated from the Church and the sacraments. She was, they said, over eighty years old. The priest himself was not quite eighty-three.

And so they began. Leaning on the strong shoulders of the two Indians, one at either side, the old priest plodded, ever so slowly, up the hill. At times they practically had to carry him.

He recited prayers all the way, often aloud. "Lord Jesus, You are the only One who can give me the strength!" The path was so narrow that the trio constantly scraped the brush on both sides. The biting wind and the dust clouds it created did not make the ascent any easier. Once the priest mused, "This trail is fit only for goats!" Just then, a wild mountain goat bounded past them and up the hilly course as if it were a super-highway. The climb took them about forty minutes. Finally, they reached the top of the small mountain. To the aged priest it seemed a miracle. "By the grace of God, I made it!"

Before him stood the old Otomi woman's *choza,* thrown together many years earlier of maguey leaves and a few sticks. One end of the brush roof had disappeared, and the merciless wind whipped through like gunfire. There, in the opposite corner, lay the woman, whining with pain and cold. The priest bent over her, tenderly heard her confession and extended to her the saving pardon of Christ. He anointed her face and hands with the Oil of the Sick, as her many relatives stood around to comfort her.

Almost immediately a sense of relief came upon the sick woman and the members of her family. Someone started a hymn of thanksgiving to the Blessed Virgin, and all joined in the singing, including the priest, who was grateful to God that he had been able to get to the top of the mountain and render this service to one of Christ's least brethren. An impish smile crossed the old priest's wrinkled face as he sang. For some reason he had remembered that day, almost thirty years before in far-off California, when a certain inborn spirit of adventure, plus a good dose of stubborn, human pride, had driven him to the top of Mount Shasta.

Two

SEEDS OF A VOCATION

Umberto Olivieri first saw the light of day at ten o'clock on Saturday morning, January 12, 1884, the second child and first son of Pietro Olivieri and Teresa Mancini Olivieri. He was born in the heart of Rome on the sixth and topmost floor of an apartment building on the Piazza dell'Esquilino in the shadow of the Basilica of Santa Marìa Maggiore, one of the great churches of the world dedicated to the Blessed Virgin Mary. He considered himself from that day under the special protection of our Blessed Mother.

Two days after his birth he was taken across the square to the basilica to be baptized. He was reborn in Christ at the hands of Don Stanìslao Freschi, one of the assistant pastors of the parish, and given the name Umberto Leone Achille Giuseppe Marìa, honoring, in order, the reigning king of Italy Umberto I, the reigning Pope Leo XIII, his maternal grandfather and godfather Achille Mancini, his paternal grandfather Giuseppe Olivieri (and the foster father of Our Lord), and the Mother of Christ. His godmother was Margherita De Guidi Olivieri, his paternal grandmother. The records of the basilica are so complete that we even know the name of the midwife who delivered him, Giacomina Fedeli.

Every priest wonders at times which of the baby boys he has baptized will grow up to become priests. Father Freschi may have wondered about little Umberto, but he could never have guessed when and under what circumstances *this* priestly vocation would bear fruit!

9

Pietro Olivieri was born in 1854 at Acqui, in northwestern Italy, of a good Piedmontese family. His father, Giuseppe, was a well-educated man. One of Giuseppe's brothers was a priest, the only known priest or religious on either side of Umberto's family until Umberto himself was ordained. About 1880 Pietro Olivieri came to Rome and met and married Teresa Mancini. He entered the service of the royal family, and at the time of Umberto's birth was secretary to the first aide-de-camp of King Umberto I. The first aide-de-camp was, you might say, the chief of the military staff of the king, holding the rank of general. The royal family, the House of Savoy, had been the rulers of Piedmont before the unification of Italy. Pietro's Piedmontese origin undoubtedly helped him to secure his position. He was also a reserve officer in the infantry. He was tall and slim, with precise military bearing. Umberto would grow up to resemble him remarkably.

The Mancinis were an old and distinguished Roman family. They claimed a relationship to the famous niece of Cardinal Mazarin, Marìa Mancini, who was in love with Louis XIV of France. Giovanni Mancini, Umberto's great-grandfather, was born about 1800. He imbibed freely of the spirit of the French Revolution, which may explain why he named his eleven children, all sons, after pagan heroes and persecutors of the Church. Little wonder, Umberto used to say, that of all those eleven sons not one entered the service of the Church. Achille, born in 1830, was the eldest. Then there were Ulisse, Settimio Severo, Tito and others. One of them, Cèsare, died as a boy. He is buried in the family plot by the entrance to the great cemetery at the Basilica of St. Lawrence outside the Walls. His grave is marked by a splendid sculpture of a sleeping, naked boy, which the Italian government would now like to put into a museum. It is an indication of the wealth of the Mancini family at that time. Strangely, those of Giovanni Mancini's eleven sons who married had no sons of their own, with the exception of Decio, whose only son died as a small child. And so the family name was lost. Achille Mancini married the Contessa Leonardi.

They became the parents of three daughters: Virginia, Italina and Teresa, born in 1859, who married Pietro Olivieri.

Pietro and Teresa were ultimately blessed with nine children. The eldest was Costanza, born in 1881. Umberto, as we have seen, arrived in 1884, followed just fifteen months later by Raimondo, called Dino. Then there were Virginia (1887), Guglielmo, called Lello (1888), Carlo (1889), Margherita (1893), Ottorino (1895) and Màssimo (1898). At this writing only Dino and Carlo are still living. Dino, who never married, followed his father into royal service, becoming the secretary first of Queen Mother Margherita, widow of Umberto I; then of Queen Elena, wife of Vittorio Emanuele III; and finally of Prince Umberto, who reigned briefly as King Umberto II and then went into exile in Portugal. Dino—Count Raimondo Olivieri—at the age of ninety, remains with the ex-king to this day. Dino and Umberto grew up together and their relationship was always very close. We shall catch up with the other Olivieris as the story progresses.

Pietro, in his position in the service of Umberto I and later of Vittorio Emanuele III, did not deal directly with the royal family. The Olivieri household was, however, always conscious of the doings of the House of Savoy, even to the point of regarding them somewhat matter-of-factly. In later years, Umberto Olivieri would enchant his own daughters with stories which seemed like fairy tales—of kings and queens, princes and princesses—as, for example, how Princess Yolanda, eldest daughter of Vittorio Emanuele III, once fell head over heels in love with their uncle Dino.

Early one morning, when Umberto was about eleven or twelve years old, he unknowingly had a race with the man for whom he was named, His Majesty Umberto I. The boy was on his way to the Church of Madonna dei Monti on the Via dei Serpenti, not far from the Colosseum. Saint Benedict Joseph Labre is buried in that church. Umberto would often visit there and then go to see an aunt who lived nearby. This day, as he was walking, he spied a fine carriage with spirited horses approaching. Why not try to outrun the horses? He ran along the side of the street as fast as his legs would carry him. When he reached the church he was still ahead. Slightly out of breath, he turned to look at the coach as it passed. There he was, King Umberto, on his way to a favorite hunting place at the edge of the city.

In 1903 Umberto and Dino went with their father to Turin. They were to spend the night in the royal palace. The custodian received them and, torch in hand, led them up the main staircase. At the top of the stairs was a huge statue of a soldier of the olden times. The flickering torchlight created a shadow effect which seemed to make the statue come to life. And there were the words: "Eugene the Great Captain." Umberto was impressed because in those days he had been reading about the wars between Austria and France, when Piedmont was allied with Austria. He also knew that Eugene's mother had been a Mancini, one of the nieces of Cardinal Mazarin. She had married a prince of Savoy. The nineteen year old went to sleep in a magnificent, tall, old-fashioned bed, his mind filled with thoughts of Eugene the Great Captain. This man was supposed to enter the service of the Church but instead chose the military life. He wanted to be in the army of the king of France, but the king turned him away. So he went instead to the other side, Austria. He led the Austrian troops in many successful battles and covered himself with glory. In the morning Umberto awoke at sunrise and saw that the first rays of the sun were falling on the Basìlica Superga, a big, beautiful church on a Turin hilltop, where the kings and princes of Piedmont are buried. All these experiences gave the boy a lasting impression of the Royal House of Savoy, an impression which he was to share with ex-King Umberto II one day many years later in far-off Mexico.

Pietro and Teresa Olivieri were not strong in their Catholic practice. Umberto acknowledged in later years that he owed the beginning of his religious education to an old family servant, Marianna. He called her his "first spiritual mother." Umberto was about twelve years of age when Marianna came to work for the

Olivieri family. She was about seventy. Marianna had been a loyal servant in the family of Umberto's grandfather Achille Mancini. Achille was a liberal and under suspicion by the government of the Papal States. When the police arrived one day at the house, Marianna knew why they were there. She ran to her master, shouting, "Signor Achille, Signor Achille, *la polizìa, la polizìa . . .* ," whereupon Signor Mancini, wearing one shoe and one slipper, darted out a back door and escaped to the kingdom of Naples.

Marianna was very kind to the Olivieri children and taught them their prayers. The children were impressed with her piety. Whenever she would reach into her pocket to give Signora Olivieri the change from the marketing, her rosary would always fall out. She taught the children how to say the rosary and instilled in them a devotion to the Holy Souls in Purgatory. She was a woman of simple faith, so there was no possibility of catechism lessons, but the essentials were there.

One day Marianna was very late in returning from the marketplace. Signora Olivieri was worried. When she finally arrived, Umberto's mother said, "Marianna, we were so afraid that you had been killed on the street!"

"Oh, no, signora," Marianna replied calmly, "don't worry. I'm not going to die on the street. I'm going to die in my own bed, with the assistance of the priest. That's the way I'm going to die."

After a couple of years' service in the Olivieri household, Marianna returned to her own home in Perugia, and shortly after she died in just the way that she had predicted.

About this time Umberto was confirmed at the Church of San Carlo ai Catinari. His sponsor was Roberto Babbano, who worked in his father's office. First Holy Communion in those days was not received until the age of twelve or thirteen. The decree of Pope Pius X on First Communion around the age of seven had not yet been promulgated. Umberto was sixteen when he received his First Communion. Aunt Virginia took him and Dino to the Barnabite Fathers, a Belgian religious order in Rome, for a week's preparation. That was all.

Umberto was not a brilliant student in the *ginnasio,* but perhaps that was because he did not always apply himself fully to the task. He failed the second year and had to repeat it, with the result that he spent six years instead of the usual five in that school, in which Latin was the principal subject. Next he enrolled in the Liceo Ennio Quirino Visconti di Roma for three years of study to prepare him to enter the university.

Young Olivieri was an avid reader. He read everything he could get his hands on. Although speculative thought had an early attraction for him, adventure stories appealed to him the most. They stirred a wanderlust which, in God's plan, would someday take him across the ocean to America, and ultimately to Mexico and the people God willed that he should serve as a priest. Once he read a story about a Swiss man who started his career as a salaried clerk, then became a newspaper editor, then a teacher and finally worked his way up in governmental service until he attained one of the highest official positions. Umberto was amazed that one person could cram so many "lives" into a single lifetime. Little did he know what God had in store for him!

He perfected his knowledge of French, which he had studied in school, by reading the French magazines that belonged to the king of Italy. Once the king had finished them, he passed them to his first aide-de-camp. The general, in turn, gave them to Umberto's father who brought them home. There were other "hand-me-downs" that were even more important—newspapers sent to His Majesty by Porfirio Díaz, dictator of Mexico. They were filled with pictures of parades and military reviews. Umberto read them with gusto. What a thrill for him to imagine that he was in that faraway land, doing battle for or against this or that group of insurgents! There always seemed to be a war on in Mexico. He had little difficulty reading the Spanish language although he had never learned it.

It was around this time, too, that Umberto first heard about Our Lady of Guadalupe, the appearance of the Blessed Virgin to Juan Diego, a humble Indian, on the hill of Tepeyac outside Mexico City in the year 1531. Something about the story appealed to the young man. "Just think! There, on the cloak of that poor Indian, is the miraculous image of our Blessed Mother, not painted by human hands. Someday I must see it for myself!"

In school Umberto had studied the famous ode by Carducci, one of his *Odi Barbare,* which speaks eloquently of the death of Maximilian, the young Austrian archduke whom Napoleon III had sent to become emperor of Mexico. His brief reign ended in 1867 on the Cerro de las Campanas, the hill of the bells, at Querétaro, where he was shot by a firing squad at the order of Benito Juárez. "What a tragedy!" thought young Olivieri. "Maximilian might have guaranteed the freedom of the Church in Mexico. He might have been able to expel the devilish forces of Masonry. Someday I must go to Querétaro and see for myself the place where this great man died!"

For as long as Umberto could remember, the Olivieri family had spent their summer holidays at Lèvanto on the Italian Riviera. The family of Costanza Olivieri Querini, his elder sister, still have a place there. Umberto particularly enjoyed swimming, while Dino favored cycling. Lèvanto was a rather primitive place when Umberto first knew it, but gradually it began to develop. One of the founders of the Fiat automobile factory in Turin built a beautiful summer home there, and he was soon followed by other aristocrats from Turin and also from Milan.

It was at Lèvanto that Umberto met his childhood sweetheart, the Contessa Costanza Viansson. They were the same age, Costanza being only four days younger. Umberto also became a pal of her brother Adolfo. Young Olivieri looked forward every summer to being with the Vianssons. When they were both several years older he asked Costanza to marry him. She refused him because he was not of the nobility. He was heartbroken. Sometime later he received a postal card:

"Dear Umberto: I am sending you this card to inform you that I am engaged to the Marchese Alessandro Valdetaro, Lieutenant of the Cavalry. We are to be married on _____ Fondest regards, Costanza."

Lucky Valdetaro, he thought.

It was painful, many years later, for Umberto to recall the fate of his old friends. Adolfo Viansson lived a riotous life and died at the age of thirty-seven. Costanza found Valdetaro unbearable. This nobleman became an utter scoundrel, falsifying his wife's signature to obtain money, defrauding the Italian military in which he held a position of trust. Eventually he had to flee to Mexico, where he became involved with a married woman. Her outraged husband killed him. Meanwhile, back in Italy, Costanza became more and more despondent. One day she threw herself out of a window. Throughout his life Umberto was to learn lessons such as these of the futility of living according to the spirit of the world. They made a deep impression on him, but the time of his real conversion was still far off.

Even more distasteful to Umberto were those who had never done anything with their lives, nothing good, nothing bad. Scripture calls them the lukewarm. "Because thou art . . . neither cold nor hot, I am about to vomit thee out of my mouth." (Rev. 3:16) Dante places in a special part of his *Inferno* those who lived *"senza infamia e senza lodo,"* "without infamy and without praise." *"Questi sciaurati, che mai non fur vivi."* (Canto III, 36, 64) They were the people who were really "never alive" at all. Umberto made up his mind that he would not be one of them.

His study of *La Divina Commedia,* required reading in Italian secondary schools, was to have a profound influence upon his life. Someday he was to teach Dante, in the original Italian, to others. He considered Dante Alighieri the greatest writer not only of Italy but of all Christian Europe.

It was while he was in the *liceo* that Umberto met his "second spiritual mother." Signora Antonietta Cerruti came from a distinguished family of Milanese silk producers. Her husband worked with Umberto's father in the service of the king. They had a pretty daughter who captured Umberto's heart for a while. Signora Cerruti, a devout woman, gave the young man a copy of *The Imitation of Christ* of Thomas a Kempis. He read it diligently. She also told him that one could go to Mass every day. This possibility had never occurred to him.

At that time the Olivieri family was living very near the Church of San Carlo alle Quattro Fontane, affectionately called San Carlino, which stands close to the Palazzo Quirinale. The small church, dating from 1640, is recognized as Bernini's first project. It is interesting to note that its measurements were kept within the dimensions of one of the pillars supporting the cupola of St. Peter's Basilica. The "four fountains" are at an intersection nearby. They are entitled "the Tiber," "the Anio," "Fidelity" and "Strength."

The boy began to attend Mass every morning, or practically every morning, at San Carlino. There he became acquainted with the Trinitarian Fathers, who were in charge of the little gem of a church. They were Spanish Basques who had served in their order's missions in South America, Chile and Peru especially. Umberto struck up a friendship with Father Antonino. There were others, too, Father Agostino and Father Carlo, but it was Father Antonino, a priest recognized for his piety, who was to have the greatest influence on the young man's life. He chose Father Antonino as his confessor and spiritual director and conferred with him almost daily. The priest impressed upon him, particularly, the importance of the virtue of chastity, both for the unmarried and for the married.

At times Umberto felt strongly inclined to enter the service of the Church and perhaps become a priest. He asked and received guidance from Father Antonino. Somedays, as he watched, devoutly, the celebrant at the altar of San Carlino, he would dream of being a priest himself and offering his first Mass at that same altar, with his mother and father and family and friends in attendance. How God must have smiled down from Heaven! Yes, someday he would be a priest, and he would celebrate his first Solemn Mass at San Carlino, but his parents would long be gone, and those in attendance would include many men and women who were not yet born.

Sometimes he would ask the Trinitarian Fathers to converse with him in Spanish. He began to entertain hopes for an appointment in the Italian diplomatic service, perhaps to Argentina. For this he would need to have a good knowledge of the Spanish language. God, of course, had His own reasons for making it possible for Umberto to become proficient in that tongue.

Big sister Costanza was married to Signor Querini, a well-to-do man. The wedding was attended by General Brusatti, first aide-de-camp of the king, and other distinguished military men. It was an element of prestige for the middle-class Olivieri family that Costanza should have made such a good marriage. In later years Umberto would regret deeply that his two younger sisters, Virginia and Margherita, neither of whom married, did not enter religious life. Their mother's sister Virginia, who also died a spinster, had been solicited several times by a French order of nuns in Rome, but she did not enter. Umberto came to feel that, had Zia Virginia become a religious, his two sisters would have followed her example.

As his years in the *liceo* drew to a close, Umberto gave much thought to his future career. He was certain of a position in the service of the royal family, but this did not interest him. The position went instead to Dino. Through his father Umberto became familiar with many army officers. He was seriously inclined toward a military career—the adventure of it attracted him—but his father was not agreeable. He studied mathematics intensely in the hope of gaining one of the relatively few nominations to the naval academy but found himself quite deficient in that subject. (Many years later he was to feel no sadness at not having become a naval officer, what with the terrible losses sustained by the Italian navy in the world wars.) And, always, there was the nagging question: should he become a priest?

Painting, also, was a great interest, as well as music and all the fine arts. When he was about seventeen years of age, Umberto showed some of his designs to the famous Senator Gavazzi and frankly asked that learned man's advice. Should he take up the brush and palette seriously, or should he devote himself to the religious life? Senator Gavazzi looked at the artwork, laughed gently, and opined that the young man would find himself more suited to the religious life.

Umberto did well in the *liceo* and graduated honorably in

1903. Shortly after his graduation, he made a trip to Acqui to meet for the first, and only, time his granduncle, Don Raimondo Olivieri. Acqui is a fair-sized provincial city in Piedmont, rather well known throughout Italy for its mud baths. Don Raimondo was a distinguished priest, a canon and archdeacon of the Acqui Cathedral who had been honored by the Pope. He had founded an order of Ursuline Sisters for social work in Acqui. He had known St. John Bosco personally. He was very kind to Pietro and Teresa Olivieri, sending an occasional five lire (worth much more then than now) to augment Pietro's salary, a gift which was welcome with nine children to rear. The family respected him greatly. Dino was named for him.

Father Raimondo received Umberto cordially, and the young man confided that he was thinking seriously of studying for the priesthood. The old priest beamed approvingly, swept his hand in the direction of his huge library, and promised, "All these books I will give to you if you become a priest!" A few years after their visit, Don Raimondo died.

The offer had been tempting, but Umberto was not sure. There were so many things he wanted to do with his life, how could he do them all? He never forgot Don Raimondo, however, and the day would come when he would pray to his heavenly granduncle for help and would credit Father Raimondo with being one of the inspirations that eventually led him to the priesthood.

Three

A SPIRIT OF ADVENTURE

Umberto's doubts about his future were temporarily resolved when, later in 1903, he enrolled at the University of Rome to pursue the study of law. He would have to learn both Roman law and Italian civil law. He would also have to master canonical law, and it would prove to be a difficult subject. This refers not to the canon law of the Church, which was not codified until 1918, but rather to the laws drawn up by the kingdom of Italy, which served as the foundation for the relationship between the State and the Church. With all of this to learn, Umberto especially wished to study economics.

His mother agreed to advance him the money to pay his expenses at the university, to be reimbursed when he was able to save enough from his future earnings. She established a strict regimen of study and obliged him to follow it. Her money was not going to be wasted! Later Umberto could look back on his mother's severity and be grateful that she kept him on the straight and narrow, but at the time he wondered why she couldn't be more gentle!

While he was following his courses at the university, he was also supposed to be preparing for a position in the administration of the government. That position could not be had for the favor of some influential person. He must win it through competitive examination.

So, for several years, it was study, *study,* STUDY! Umberto had a room separate from the rest of the family in the apartment near San Carlino. Mother Olivieri made him "crack the books" all day, every day, with the exception of the hours two or three times a week when he went to attend lectures at the university. She permitted him to go out after sunset. As a matter of fact, to conserve precious oil—there were only oil lamps, no electricity—she did not want him studying at night. She seemed pleased if he chose to visit the Fathers at San Carlino.

Actually, practically every day, the young law student would go out early in the morning, also. At half past five or six o'clock he would attend Mass at San Carlino and perhaps have a word with Father Antonino. Then he would take a long walk for some much-needed exercise. He loved to go walking on the Parioli, a great avenue which at that time was out in the country but is now all built up. Then he would go down along the river, the Tiber, to the Piazza del Pòpolo, and finally come home by way of the Via Sistina. As far as Umberto knew, his mother never discovered that he was taking those early morning walks.

In preparation for his governmental position, Umberto followed the courses in constitutional law given by Professor Luigi Luzzatti at the University of Rome. The lecturer was widely known as an Italian economist and had served several times as minister of the treasury and premier of Italy. After three failures Olivieri finally passed the competitive examinations in constitutional law and administrative law. He ranked tenth among the 350 successful applicants, which pleased his parents very much.

So, in 1906, Umberto Olivieri went to work for the Treasury Department. It was nine to five, day in and day out, with half an hour for lunch, and he hated it! There must be more to life than this. No romanticism, no adventure, no challenge! Well, the only thing to do was to stick with it and hope that it might lead to something better. Perhaps it would be a spring-board to a nomination to the diplomatic corps. Ah, to go to South America! Or to the United States! To the United States? But he knew no English. Something would have to be done about that.

God saw to it that Umberto's path crossed that of Mr. Walter O'Neill, a retired English gentleman of Irish background, who was living in Rome in the service of the Pope. He had made money as an industrialist in Liverpool and had been rewarded with a papal knighthood for his generosity to the Church. Now he was living out his life, quietly, doing whatever the Vatican would ask of him. He had plenty of time and was anxious to occupy it usefully. With no reluctance, therefore, he agreed to teach English to the five or six young Italian men who approached him. There were Vittorio Puccinelli and a fellow named De Santis (both of whom later became doctors), Toccafondi and perhaps one other whose name was lost to memory, and there were Dino and Umberto. O'Neill patiently taught them English grammar three times a week for six months. He always served tea and cookies in his apartment on the Via Sistina. He would, of course, take nothing for his services.

Umberto devoured every book in English that he could find. Zia Virginia was also studying English at the time, and he went through all her readers. He read the life of Henry Morton Stanley, the British explorer of Africa, but this only increased his wanderlust. He felt a kinship to Stanley, who also had less than a tender relationship with his mother. Back at the office, there was a co-worker named Matteucci who had lived a year in England. Umberto would frequently spend his brief lunch hour with Matteucci, who helped him to improve his skill in the language.

And then there was the Pensione Bethel. Umberto could hardly wait until five o'clock. He dashed home, cleaned up, changed his clothes, hopped on a streetcar and went down to this little hotel to enjoy the evening with the American girls who came there to spend the winter in Rome. Mabel Curry, from a fine Boston family, was his favorite. He would have liked to marry Mabel. But at least she helped him with his English. The other fellows from Mr. O'Neill's class often went with him to the Pensione Bethel.

In a sense Olivieri was happy with his job. It gave him a certain independence. He kept on with his work at the university, but now he was able to pay his own expenses. He also found time to undertake a thorough study of the Constitution of the United States, for by now he was convinced that America was somehow in his future.

Mountain climbing and hunting were his principal recreations at this time. As often as he could, he compensated for the drudgery of the office by escaping into the great outdoors. In September 1906 he was staying for a few days at a mountain place east of Rome called Bellegra, where there is an old Franciscan monastery. Three other young men joined him, and the four took a hike from Bellegra to Subiaco, down in the valley of the river Anio, something like twenty kilometers. They went for a refreshing swim in the river. Umberto was nearly drowned when he was carried away by the swift current. Just before he would have been swept over a steep drop, he managed to grab a stone outcropping and catapult himself onto dry land. God did not want to call him to heaven yet, at least not in this place. He had other plans for the valley of Subiaco in the life of Umberto Olivieri.

The men dressed themselves and proceeded into the little town of Subiaco and on to the Benedictine monastery of Santa Scolàstica. Nearby is the Sacro Speco, a cave in which St. Benedict had lived fourteen centuries before. They were met at the door of Santa Scolàstica by a pleasant, young priest-monk. He introduced himself as Dom Simone Lorenzo Salvi, master of novices, and offered them hospitality in the name of Christ. Leading the young men to the refectory, he seated them and saw that they were served a nice lunch. Then he accompanied them to the door and smilingly bade them farewell. Father Salvi and Umberto Olivieri would meet again, right there at Santa Scolàstica, but half a century would pass in the meantime. The circumstances of their next meeting, had God revealed them on that day in September 1906, would have stunned both men and left them shaking their heads in disbelief.

It must have been about the same time, or perhaps a year later but also in the autumn, that an amusing incident took place. All his life Umberto loved to tell the story, and his children never tired of hearing it. He must have used it in public, too, for a typewritten copy, in English, was found among his effects. We'll let him tell it in his own words, but first, a little background information.

After the death of his wife, the Contessa Leonardi, Achille Mancini, who had failed in his business and lost most of his holdings and almost all of his money, went to live in the old castle of San Vittorino, which belonged to the Mancini family. He died there in 1901. Umberto went with his mother and father and other relatives to bring back the body for interment in the family monument. All the way to Rome, Uncle Settimio, one of the brothers of the deceased, kept telling seventeen-year-old Umberto "ghost stories" about the castle, which was supposedly haunted. The impressionable teenager never forgot that day.

The Ghost in the Castle

"The story I am going to tell really happened to me. I could have been the unfortunate victim of the ghosts in an old castle . . . but let's not anticipate.

"When I was a young man, about twenty-two or twenty-three years old, I had an old aunt who was the heiress to a remnant of a large estate which belonged to the family of my grandfather. It was situated in a little town near Rome, called San Vittorino, not very far from Tìvoli. I used to go there once a year to collect some rents from my aunt's tenants. I got there by a steam train of diminutive size which went from Rome to Tìvoli. I would leave the train at Ponte Lucano, the old bridge across the River Anio. The spot is famous inasmuch as, right by the bridge, there is one of the mausoleums of the early Roman times, reduced into a stronghold for defense against the enemies of the city of Tìvoli.

"Leaving the train I would walk across the plain and then penetrate into a dale made by the *contrafforti* of the Prenestinian Hills which limit the Roman Campagna on the northeast side. I had to walk about two hours before I could reach the deep natural moat which is part of the defensive system of the little borough of San Vittorino. The main stronghold of the place was constituted by the castle, not too imposing in size, but massively built as to represent a serious obstacle against any attack of marauders, brigands or soldiers of venture.

"On a certain day in the late September of some fifty years ago [he must have been writing in the late 1950s], I arrived at San Vittorino about five o'clock in the afternoon. I spoke to the tenants of my aunt and attended to the business of the collection of the moneys due. After settling the business part of my excursion, I requested these same people to find a place where I could eat and sleep.

"Being very fond of hunting I thought of taking a few shots at the quail in the surrounding fields, for which purpose I had carried my double-barreled gun. While I was talking to the tenants, I noticed that a pointer had come close to me and seemed to be rather interested in me because I was carrying a gun. I thought that it would be very desirable to be assisted by the dog and, in order to be certain of his friendship for me, I gave him some bread and patted him on the head. That was sufficient to establish an excellent friendship. I enticed him to go with me and he responded very willingly.

"We crossed the moat on the other side of the town and soon were in a large stubble plain. No sooner had we arrived there than a big, fat quail jumped out and was immediately felled. The dog was greatly animated by this success, and in a little over an hour I had bagged four fat quail. As the sun was going down, and in those times the land was infested by malaria, I returned to the town for my supper and a much desired rest.

"I was a little dismayed when, inquiring if they had found a room and a bed for me, I was told by the tenants that they had prepared a bed in the old castle, which was completely uninhabited for a long time. The idea of sleeping in the castle did not please me because, besides the smell and dust of an old building, I had the sad memory of my grandfather, who had died in that very place several years before. All the details of his death came back to my mind, and I did not cherish the thought of a night in such a gloomy spot. However, I didn't want to show any sign of fear to my hosts and, looking at my faithful pointer, I thought that it would be a fine thing if the dog stayed with me.

"For this purpose, I kept him with me for supper, giving him some tidbits of the lamb chops that made my repast. The friendship between me and my canine companion seemed to be firmly established. When came the moment of retiring, I made sure that he would come with me to the castle.

"I fell into bed like a log, but during my sleep in the early part of the night, I heard a terrific noise which sounded like doors banging and chairs falling. My sleepiness was too heavy for me to get up and see what it was, and anyway I trusted in the dog. To tell the truth, I was a little afraid. The noise soon subsided and I turned over and went back to sleep. But again, a little later, I was awakened by the same noise. This time I realized that the dog had something to do with it because he was running around the room. Again I fell fast asleep and did not pay much attention when I heard the noise again. The last part of the night was quiet.

"I finally woke up when the sun was high in the sky. I felt pleased that the ghosts had not removed my bed. Rubbing my eyes to recognize my surroundings, I was very glad to see that the dog was sleeping quietly, but all around there was clear evidence that the poor beast had had something to do with the ghosts. Scattered around the room there were no less than *nine* enormous rats, all cold and stiff. The battle had been hard, the victory complete. Chairs and tables were out of place, but the dog seemed satisfied with his duty fulfilled.

"Needless to say, I was more than happy for my friendship with the pointer, and I thought that probably the soul of my grandfather had kept vigil over me so that no harm should befall me."

Olivieri had been able to defer his compulsory military service because of his studies at the university. In 1908 he decided to fulfill his obligation. He hoped to be sent to Naples for basic training. He had been taking a few singing lessons in Rome, to develop his naturally beautiful tenor voice, and now he was anxious to experience the feeling of Neapolitan song in the surroundings of its origin. To Naples he was sent.

Ah, romantic Nàpoli! The gorgeous bay, the enchanting islands, breathtaking Sorrento, ominous Vesuvius, the splendid ruins of Pompeii! But there was work, too. For one thing, he had to learn to march in step. After many years he could still remember a few lines of one of the silly marching songs:

> *Brodo, sempre brodo,*
> *Pasta asciutta mi fa male,*
> *Caporale, caporale . . .*

Though the typical army fare was scarcely gourmet quality, Umberto did enjoy his military service at Naples. He stayed there ten months and advanced rapidly from buck private to corporal to sergeant. Fencing was a special thrill for him. He became friendly with his captain, a well-educated man with an air of elegance who helped make military life exciting and pleasurable. But the peer influence was strong, alas, and Umberto did not always conduct himself in a manner befitting a Christian.

He passed the examination for appointment as a second lieutenant in the field artillery reserve. He requested to be sent to Florence or Pavia or Milan because he had friends in northern Italy, and then he returned to Rome to await his appointment.

The young second lieutenant was sent to Florence in 1909. Papà Olivieri used his influence with the officers of the royal household to secure lodging for Umberto in an upstairs room of the Palazzo Pitti, once the residence of the grand duke of Tuscany. It was elegant! How envious the other young lieutenants were!

It was at this time that Umberto's portrait, in military uniform, was painted by a dear friend of the family, Arnaldo Tamburini the younger. The portrait is now the property of the art gallery of the University of Santa Clara. Umberto loved the Tamburinis. The father, also named Arnaldo, was a well-known painter, and the son was following in his father's footsteps. These people, thought Umberto, are really doing something with their lives.

Umberto loved horseback riding, and there was plenty of that. In the summer time the regiment went with horses and guns to a place of encampment. One day at practice he was injured when his left foot was run over by the wheel of a gun. To strengthen it he went climbing in the nearby mountains but twisted the same foot very badly. So he was laid up for a while but fortunately recovered completely. Once, in winter time, he was riding his favorite horse along the river Arno. Horse and rider sank into deep mud. It could have been a tragic situation, especially for the terrified horse, but somehow, by the grace of God, they managed to extricate themselves.

Pietro Olivieri may have secured regal lodgings for his son, but he did not indulge the young officer's every fancy. Umberto went shopping in Florence for clothes, more a matter of necessity than luxury. He ran up a bill that was far beyond his means to pay. "Papà will take care of it." Papà would not! Umberto was forced to go to other relatives to borrow the money, and it would be a long time before he would be able to free himself from the burden of debt. To his credit, he eventually repaid every cent.

Umberto stayed twelve months in Florence. Social life was very pleasant. One of his frequent dates was Giuseppina Tamburini, of the artists' family. His friend Captain Nobili would take him to the Pensione Piccioli, a small hotel on the bank of the Arno near the Ponte Santa Trinità, operated by the captain's mother-in-law, where frequently there were American guests. Umberto had many chances to use his English. There, one day, he was introduced to Agnes Kent.

She was young and lovely. A delightful conversationalist, with plenty of good-humored patience for his broken English. And there was something about her eyes that made her especially attractive. Delicately almond-shaped, with almost an Oriental cast. Umberto enjoyed being with Agnes. Agnes was enchanted by this gay, witty, tall, handsome lieutenant with the striking Roman profile. She was traveling abroad with her mother and three sisters. They came from Bronxville, New York. One day they all went to see Umberto at his "barracks," the Pitti Palace. Needless to say, they were overwhelmed by the magnificence that surrounded them.

As Agnes and her family traveled around Italy, Umberto always seemed to be at the various railway stations ahead of them with a bouquet of roses in hand. How exciting to be wooed in the Old World manner! The time came for the Kents to return to America. Agnes and Umberto said good-bye. They both expressed the fond hope that they might meet again.

Early in 1910 Lieutenant Olivieri completed his military service and went back to Rome. He put the finishing touches on his major thesis in economics on "English and German Protectionism to Shipping Trusts." He wrote two lesser papers, one in civil law, the other in Roman law. His work was accepted. The University of Rome awarded him the degree Doctor of Jurisprudence *in utroque juro.* He passed the bar examination and was thus entitled to practice as an attorney. He chose not to do so. He would stay in his position with the Treasury Department and hope that his legal knowledge would help him to advance.

In 1911 the Kents came again to Italy. Agnes and Umberto were delighted to see each other again. Umberto struck up a firm friendship with Mr. Kent. William Winthrop Kent came from a good family of Bangor, Maine. He was a distinguished architect and author. His books covered such diverse subjects as ancient and modern architectural wrought iron, hooked rugs, and the hardware—knobs, handles, etc.—of antique furniture. His brother Edward, who was to die a hero's death in the sinking of the *Titanic,* was also an accomplished architect. W. W. Kent's wife, Jessie, had deep roots in American history. She was a member of the Adams family, which gave the United States its second and sixth presidents.

It came as little surprise to either family when Agnes Kent and Umberto Olivieri announced their engagement. The Kents, of course, were Protestants. Umberto, though he had lost the

fervor of his youthful visits to San Carlino, was still too much
a Catholic to settle for anything other than marriage by a
priest. Agnes was agreeable and consented to raise as Catholics
any children with whom God might bless them. The wedding
date was not, however, set immediately.

The young lawyer greatly enjoyed touring places of historical
and architectural importance in the company of Mr. Kent. The
older man was well acquainted with Italy's monuments. Each
was able to show the other hitherto unfamiliar spots. The Kents
took Umberto on a trip through central Italy, visiting particularly
Assisi and Perugia. Umberto was embarrassed that he did not
own a better pair of trousers, but he did not have much money
in those days. Now, they were in Perugia and were going to the
fancy Hotel Baglioni. His trousers were all torn in back.
What could he do? He remembered that Marianna, the old
servant who taught him his childhood prayers, had lived in
Perugia. Of course, Marianna had been dead for several years,
but surely there was someone who could help him. He went to
Marianna's house and prevailed upon one of her nieces to stitch
up his trousers. There! He no longer had to feel self-conscious
in the presence of his future in-laws.

Agnes and her family returned to America, and she and
Umberto corresponded faithfully for eight or nine months.
Finally, the date of their marriage was set. And it was going
to take place in Massachusetts. At last, Umberto would see the
United States, if only for a few days!

He was seasick all the way over. The boat landed in New
York on July 29, 1912. Some Italian friends of the Kents
met him, and soon he was on his way to Boston. The wedding,
since it was a marriage of mixed religion, could not (in those
days) take place inside a Catholic church. The couple did not
want the cold atmosphere of the priest's rectory or the church
sacristy. So it was arranged that the wedding would be celebrated
on August 19 in the living room of the Kents' summer home
on Cape Cod. The local Catholic pastor officiated. When he
asked them, "Do you take this woman (this man) for better or
for worse until death do you part?" Umberto and Agnes each
answered, lovingly, "I do."

The newlyweds embarked for Europe only a week after their marriage. Again Umberto was seasick all the way. Agnes was sympathetic but also a little amused. She knew that her husband had at one time given serious thought to becoming an officer of the Royal Navy of Italy! They landed at Calais and immediately hired a horse and carriage for their honeymoon. For several months they traveled at a leisurely pace through France, Belgium, Holland, Germany, and Switzerland. Along the way they collected furnishings for their home, all antiques. Mr. Kent had given them a generous wedding present to help them get started in their new life. They would see a lovely credenza. It was bought and stowed in the carriage. Perhaps there would be a finely carved occasional chair. The same. When the carriage became too full, they would have its contents crated and shipped to Rome. Once they spied an old *contadina* seated on an elegant bench. They paid her, and the bench, too, went into the carriage. Finally, they arrived at Rome.

Their first home was to be a lovely apartment in the Palazzo Bianchi on the Via Salaria. What fun they had in putting their new-old furniture in place! Nothing matched, of course, but that was the way Agnes wanted it. Actually, they did manage to acquire a beautiful pre-Victorian dining-room set with matching table and chairs. The feet were carved into the cloven hoofs of an animal.

Umberto returned to his work. By now he was an under-secretary of the Treasury Department. He seldom attended Sunday Mass anymore. Agnes loved living in Rome. The Eternal City was the city of her dreams. Umberto saw that she met all the right people. The day came that she was to be presented to Queen Elena at the Royal Palace. It was a story-book come to life! Agnes curtsied properly, just as she had been instructed. Umberto had been told that he was to make three bows. In his nervousness he made four!

Then came 1914 and World War I. Italy had not yet decided to join the Allies, but Umberto, as a reserve officer, was ready at a moment's notice to serve his country. By early 1915 the tension was so heavy in Rome that one could almost hear the rumble of the guns.

Four

GOD PROVIDES

First, there was the rumble that seemed to come from the very bowels of the earth.

Giuseppina Tarquini, not quite five years of age, was happily playing with her sister Benedetta, two years younger, in an upstairs bedroom of their home at San Benedetto dei Marzi, a village near the city of Avezzano in the Abruzzi region of central Italy. Their baby sister, Erminia, slept peacefully in her crib. Their handsome, young father was also asleep, which was unusual for him on a weekday morning. Vincenzo Tarquini was a farmer. It was about eight o'clock on Wednesday, January 13, 1915. The sun was shining brightly on that winter day. Vincenza D'Arpizio Tarquini, pregnant with their fourth child, was busily preparing breakfast in the downstairs kitchen. There would be many mouths to feed. According to the custom of the time and place, this was the home of an extended family. A total of sixteen relatives shared the grand, three-story stone house.

First, there was the rumble. Vincenzo bolted awake and grabbed Giuseppina.

Then, there was the sound of shattered glass and of stone falling upon stone. Benedetta's limp form flew past them in the air. The earth convulsed again, and Giuseppina was wrenched from her father's grasp.

Then, there was the sound of his voice, "Giuseppina, Giuseppina . . ."

Then, there was silence.

In Rome, far to the west, Umberto and Agnes Olivieri were at breakfast. The night before there had been a dinner party to celebrate Umberto's thirty-first birthday. The house trembled. They sat bewildered. The building began to swing like a pendulum. They ran to the door frame, threw their arms around each other and said good-bye, knowing not if they would meet again in this life.

Word quickly reached Rome of the destruction of Avezzano and its environs. Fifty thousand soldiers were marshaled to rescue the living and bury the dead. Civilian volunteers were needed to supplement the teams. Umberto hastened to respond. He equipped himself with blanket, bandages, spade, shovel and sufficient food to sustain him for two days. Thursday evening he boarded a freight train. It took seven hours to reach Avezzano, high in the rugged Apennines.

The devastation was unbelievable. History records the Avezzano earthquake as one of the world's great natural catastrophes. Thirty thousand dead is a conservative estimate. Scarcely a building remained standing. Everywhere could be heard the desperate cries of the trapped. Horses and cows lay dead and dying alongside human victims. Wild dogs and rats prowled the ruins relentlessly. Only emergency medical treatment could be given at the scene. The injured were loaded onto trains and taken to Rome.

Pope Benedict XV made provision to care for orphans. King Vittorio Emanuele III personally led a rescue squad to the stricken area. Queen Elena worked among the refugees unloaded at the railway station in Rome. With her were hundreds of women volunteers, including Agnes Olivieri. She wrote to her family in New York, "It is the first time I ever did any good in my life and I thank God I have the chance now." Rome's hospitals were soon strained beyond capacity, and the injured had to be treated right on the floor of the train sheds. "Rome is a great hospital," wrote Agnes. "Everyone's heart must either open or turn to stone these days."

Umberto came back to Rome on Saturday, but only to replenish his emergency equipment and supplies. He had scarcely slept for three days, but he felt good. He had saved six people alive. By Sunday he was on his way again to the Abruzzi. He saw a girls' school where 300 students had lived. Only two were rescued, and they also died. This trip he was assigned to San Benedetto, where he divided his time between digging for buried victims and manning one of the food relief stations of the Red Cross. A Rome newspaper reported, "To Lawyer Olivieri was entrusted the care of the babies."

Giuseppina Tarquini lay three days and three nights in the ruins of her home. Mercifully, she was unconscious most of the time. A severe tremor at three o'clock on the morning of the second day jolted her awake and threw her onto her back, with her foot pinned beneath her. Everything was so terribly dark. Then, later, the fire reached the little girl. The pain was excruciating for a time, but soon kind oblivion overcame her. It was Saturday that a soldier began digging in the debris of the Tarquini home. His shovel struck Giuseppina's head and brought her to her senses. She looked up at him and saw a smile cross his haggard face. After burying so many dead he had found a child alive! She was not reassured. In her fright she wanted to cry out but she could not make a sound. Her mouth was filled with rubble.

The soldier rushed the badly injured girl to the aid station where she was given emergency care and identified. Periodically she was carried to the food dispensary for Nestlé's milk and crackers. There, Sunday, she looked up into the face of Umberto Olivieri. His eyes told her that she no longer need be afraid.

For several days Olivieri continued his rescue work and the feeding of the children. Now and then Giuseppina would be brought to him. Always she gazed at him with trust and longing, though no word passed her lips. There were so many children, all hungry, all wounded, all needing him, but there was something about this particular child that appealed to the deepest and best within him.

At length he prepared to return to Rome. But he could not

depart without seeing that little girl once more. The lines of a poem by Ada Negri, which he had learned in elementary school, came vividly to his mind. The poetess wrote of an abandoned child calling out to the human heart. Umberto remembered the lapses and excesses of his young manhood. He thought of the child who would never bear his name. No, he could not leave. Frantically he searched the tents, row by row, cot by cot. Finally he found Giuseppina.

Love flowed between them. She knew he would come back. Now he must find out something about her. She was sitting on the lap of a Signora di Gènova, a farmer's wife of the village. "Her name is Giuseppina Tarquini," the lady responded. "Her mother and father and all her immediate family were killed. She is the only one left. That man over there, he is her cousin."

Umberto knew what he must do. He and Agnes had been married over two years but they had no children. The doctor had told Agnes that, for physical reasons, she was unlikely to bear a child. Umberto showed his excellent credentials to the cousin and begged to be allowed to take the little orphan back with him to Rome. Signor Vincenzino D'Arpizio thought a moment. "Yes," he said, "I think that would be a fine idea. Her family are all gone. She has only distant relatives, and we have our own families to think about. She comes from a good country family. Her parents were not peasants. She would make you a good daughter."

"Do you want to go to Rome with Signor Olivieri?" D'Arpizio asked Giuseppina.

At long last the little girl spoke. "Oh, yes, I do!" She smiled at Umberto and called him "Zizi," a colloquialism for "uncle." It would always be her pet name for him.

He tenderly wrapped her in his blanket, by now soiled and worn. She could not walk, but her tiny frame was a light burden indeed. He quickly settled matters with the local authorities. They boarded a *carro bestiame,* a cattle car, the only space available. Umberto sat on the bare wooden floor, with his precious child cradled in his arms.

There was a police control at the railway station in Rome, but luckily Umberto spotted a friend who made it possible for him to proceed with the child without delay. At three o'clock in the morning of Thursday, January 21, Umberto carried Giuseppina up the wide marble staircase of the Palazzo Bianchi. Agnes was awake and waiting. With tears of joy she embraced him and kissed his tired, unshaven face. "Look!" he exclaimed. "I've brought you our first child!" Agnes looked, and her eyes, too, told Giuseppina that she had nothing to fear. They gently placed her on the sofa, and she fell at once into a sound sleep. She had found love.

After sunrise the Olivieris called a doctor to examine the little girl. Together they cut away her tattered clothing and bathed her infected wounds. Most serious were a fractured skull and a deep burn on her thigh. For the next several days she ran a high fever as she fought meningitis and tetanus. Agnes, drawing on the experience of her work at the train sheds, carefully cleansed and dressed the child's wounds daily, under the close supervision of the doctor. She wrote to her parents in America, without realizing the prophecy of her words, that the five year old in her bandages looked "like a little nun."

The youngster gradually regained her health, with the exception of a paralysis of her legs, caused by the burn, the position in which she had lain so long, and a congenitally dislocated hip. She could walk only with assistance. "She will always be a little lame, we think," wrote Agnes. The new mother and father grew to love her dearly. Her curly black hair, her flashing black eyes, her chubby little hands, her sweet disposition, her obvious affection for them charmed them utterly. They could not bear the thought of parting with her. Italian law, they found, precluded the possibility of adoption. Umberto could and would ask to be appointed her guardian until she reached the age of eighteen. The paperwork would take several months. They would call her Susanna, or Susie, but in this account we shall refer to her by her baptismal name, the name by which she is known today, Giuseppina, Josephine.

On Sunday, February 7, Umberto Olivieri returned to San Benedetto for five days. A heavy winter had set in, and the ruins were covered by snow. He carefully probed the debris of the Tarquini home for anything that might be of value to Josephine. It was then, Agnes wrote, that "he . . . tenderly wrapped up the bodies of Baby's father, . . . her two little sisters and other relatives, then himself nailed together the wood for coffins. Her mother had been buried before he came." He found a few keepsakes among the ashes and rubble. These would be for Josephine when she was older. He took final steps to assure the legality of his guardianship.

Early in March Umberto was recalled to active duty as a first lieutenant of the field artillery. He was happy to be sent to Florence and made plans to rent a room at the Pensione Piccioli, where he and Agnes had first met. There he could be sure of comfort and good food, and also he would have an opportunity to help the Picciolis. Nineteen fifteen was a bad year for hotels and stores in Italy. The war had practically nullified tourism in Europe. Furthermore, unemployment in Italy was reaching serious proportions. Agnes and Josephine joined Umberto in Florence shortly after his arrival. There the child received electric therapy for traumatic paralysis. It proved quite beneficial. How long they would be able to stay was another matter. War might be declared at any moment.

Italy joined the Allies in May. Umberto was sent to the eastern front, the Carso, where the Italians were desperately trying to dislodge the Austrian troops from their natural stronghold. He went into the war without receiving the sacraments, without even making the sign of the cross, so indifferent had he become to the practice of his faith. The fervor of his late teenage years and early twenties and the counsel of Father Antonino had faded from his conscious mind.

Agnes and Josephine returned to their home in the Eternal City. The documents for Umberto's guardianship of the orphan girl were soon ready to be finalized. Through the influence of Pietro Olivieri, Agnes secured a safe-conduct pass and brought the papers right to the front for her husband's signature. That this unusual privilege was granted is all the more remarkable for the fact that the woman was not an Italian.

On August 15, 1915, Lieutenant Olivieri participated in what could have been a decisive battle on the Carso front. He was, in fact, chiefly responsible for the planning of the advance. His artillery unit was protecting an infantry brigade comprising the twenty-fifth and twenty-sixth regiments. The Austrians were entrenched on the other side of a ridge. Somewhere behind them, theoretically, was a machine-gun unit guarding their position. How to conquer that ridge? Umberto studied the terrain carefully. His experience as a hunter had sharpened his sight. It wasn't long before he discovered a ravine through which the Italian infantry could advance. He hastened to explain his plan to the commanding general.

"All right," said the general, "you work out the strategy with Lieutenant Trombetti, the commander of the infantry company."

The two lieutenants rehearsed the operation. "Don't worry," explained Olivieri, "we'll be covering you. When you get to the head of the gulch, turn to the right and take all the trenches from the top. The enemy artillery won't be able to do anything. They can't shoot at their own soldiers."

Cautiously, Trombetti and his men forged up the ravine. The Austrian artillery began firing. But, as fortune would have it, a little puff of smoke disclosed the location of their machine-gun emplacement. Olivieri's men returned the fire and wiped out the entire unit. The Italian company reached the top and, with little difficulty, captured the position. Eight officers, 500 men and their guns were taken.

The Italian general, unfortunately, had not realized the importance of the position. He was not prepared for such a rapid advance. Had there been two battalions of Alpine soldiers, two or three thousand men, ready to move ahead into the captured territory, the Austrians would have been forced to retreat, and a new front would have been established. The Italians were at least able to hold the position, but the full potential of it was not exploited. By the time reinforcements arrived it was too late. The Austrians had the opportunity to bring in additional soldiers to prevent further advance.

A day or two later the Italian officers held a meeting. Olivieri urged the general to move the headquarters. It was likely to be hit by an Austrian zone shot. His warning was not heeded. The next morning at daybreak the enemy began firing again. The first shot seriously wounded the commanding general. His aide-de-camp was also injured; the telephonist, the veterinarian and four or five others were killed. The doctor and Lieutenant Olivieri were the only two in the command to escape unharmed. Umberto wondered why his general could not have been more like the great Russian general whose life and exploits he had studied avidly as a young man. General Skobelev was known for his trust of his junior officers and men. He always consulted them before making a decision in battle.

Probably 25,000 Italian soldiers lost their lives in that part of the front, from cholera as well as battle injuries. Shortly after the battle of August 15, Lieutenant Olivieri was hospitalized for complete exhaustion. He remained in the hospital about two months and then was granted a leave to return to his home and family in Rome.

(In November 1972, in the rectory living room of the parish of St. John the Baptist in El Cerrito, California, Father Umberto Olivieri relived every detail of the battle on the Carso as if it had taken place one year instead of fifty-seven years earlier. In his later life he came to have a great horror of the game that is war, although he still admitted the necessity of defending one's country against attack. The United States' involvement in Viet Nam made him ashamed to be an American citizen. Even though he was always bitterly anti-Communist he viewed that war, still going on at the time, as a genocidal persecution by the white race against the yellow.)

At the expiration of his sick leave, Lieutenant Olivieri was ordered to the depot of his regiment, the twenty-first Field Artillery, at Piacenza. One morning there was a request for volunteers for the *Batterìa di Montagna,* the mountain artillery.

These specially trained soldiers, with their guns carried by mules, would accompany the infantry to the northern front, the Trentino, high among the rugged Alps. Umberto was thrilled at the chance. Piacenza was foggy and gloomy. He had been feeling terribly depressed. "Why not? I've had a certain amount of preparation for mountain combat. I'm not accomplishing anything here. I might as well go and risk my life with the mountain artillery."

He was sent instead to the depot of the Third Artillery in the steep hills near Genoa. His job was to train soldiers for the mountain battery and especially to instruct them in the use of the bayonet. But perhaps he would still have his opportunity. He knew that he was due for a promotion to captain. There was a good chance that he would be sent into the Alps in command of an artillery unit, including some of these same men that he had prepared. The bulletin arrived. There was no notice of his promotion. A telephone call was placed to the division commander at Genoa. The general was adamant. "If Lieutenant Olivieri did not receive the promotion to captain, he is not to go to the front." The battery was ready to leave. A young officer, not much more than twenty-two years old, was placed in command. Strangely, he, too, was only a lieutenant. Umberto smarted at the arbitrariness of the decision.

One week later the bulletin came with the nomination of Lieutenant Olivieri to the rank of captain. He called the division commander and asked if now he might go. "No, that battery is already gone. It is too late." Divine Providence spoke with the stern words of the general. The battery that Olivieri would have commanded was totally obliterated by the Austrians. The major commanding the group of three batteries displayed remarkable bravery, staying with his guns until they were all destroyed and he himself was killed. He was awarded a gold medal posthumously. Very few of the group were saved. The young lieutenant's body was never found. It probably fell into a gulch and was covered by the snow. Umberto Olivieri got down on his knees and gave thanks to God. His place, but for a week's delay in the promotion, would have been the place of that lieutenant. It was not long after this incident that Umberto returned to the sacraments and, for a while, to a more regular, if not fervent, practice of his faith.

Captain Olivieri enjoyed Genoa, with its favorable climate. His wife and the little girl, who was now as their very own, joined him there for a time. Josephine remembers Genoa:

"Often I would go with Father when he reviewed the troops. One day, mounted on his beautiful horse, he stood at the top of a sand bank. I was perched in front of him, secure in his strong grasp. It thrilled me to see the long line of soldiers on horseback at the top of the bank. At the sound of the whistle they were to ride straight down holding themselves and the horses erect. Should one make repeated blunders or fail in some act of discipline, Father would blow his whistle with no uncertain strength and impose a penalty. One day, seeing a poor fellow tumble and roll miserably, I blew the whistle and with enthusiasm called out: 'Three days in the brig for you!' Father turned me around and faced me sternly, and with voice loud enough to be heard by his men who were enjoying the joke immensely, said: 'Who gave you permission to give orders for the captain?' He then dismissed his men and off we trotted home in complete silence. When there I received my sentence. 'Three days in the brig for you!' When I was 'released' from my days confined away from military duty, he explained that authority is to be respected and to be exercised only if delegated.

"One day when he was on leave, we went to Anzio for a few days. He put me in a boat, made large sand bags which he packed around me from the waist down to keep me from falling over backwards. He then gave me a pair of oars and had me row with all my might and main. When I would weaken, he would command: 'Forza!' ('Keep going!'). Sometimes he would say: 'Coraggio! avanti!' ('Courage! forward!'). My legs were practically useless, but he wished me to develop the rest of my body. He was also determined that I should learn to swim, in spite of the fact that I could do so only with my arms. The big waves frightened me. He tried to make me understand that I should trust him implicitly, but I remained discouragingly reluc-

tant. This, in a little girl of seven, he could not tolerate. One
day he placed me on his back. I put my arms around his neck
and held on for dear life as he, with long, powerful strokes, made
straight out for the rocks. From them he dove, holding me
securely. When we surfaced, I yelled, screamed and sputtered.
With feigned surprise he asked the reason for my strange be-
havior. 'I'm afraid!' I said over and over again. 'Afraid, when
you are with your father who loves you?' Another plunge into the
beautiful Mediterranean punctuated his words. My protest continued more vociferous than ever. Finally I gave up the battle.
It was then, and only then, that he said to me: 'Remember,
where there are trust and love, there is no room for fear.' "

Though the war had not ended, Olivieri was recalled to the
Treasury Department in Rome soon after his promotion to the
captaincy. There was important work to be done, the liquidation
of the pensions for the widows and orphans of the soldiers
killed in the war. His legal expertise was needed. By reason
of his years of service he was named first secretary. Also, he
was honored with a knighthood and authorized to use the title
Cavaliere.

Mountain climbing again became a passion for Umberto. He
loved to climb Monte Gennaro, a prominent peak dominating the
plain around Rome. From Marcellina he would go to the valley
of Licenza on the other side of the mountain, a beautiful
valley mentioned in one of the odes of Horace. He saw the
caves where, in olden times, snow from the winter's fall would
be stored, later to be brought by mule to Rome and made into
cooling refreshments.

In the valley of Licenza lived Giovanni Pupà, whom Umberto
would visit on occasion. A bloodcurdling story is told of this man.
His father had been what was called in the American West a
cattle rustler, and Giovanni was the owner of numerous head
of cattle. The wolves, which in those days infested the mountains,
were taking a tremendous toll of his livestock. Giovanni vowed
revenge. For some unknown reason he refused to use a gun.
Instead he set traps for the wolves. One day he discovered one
in a trap. He ran to the wolf to dispatch it with his hatchet.

The frightened animal bolted away, carrying the trap. Giovanni gave chase. The wolf came to a stone wall, marking a property line. Encumbered by the trap it could not jump. Giovanni split its head with his hatchet, opened the chest with his knife and ate the raw heart of the wolf on the spot.

On one visit Olivieri lamented, "Ah, Giovanni, you have eleven children and I have none. My wife cannot have a child." "Oh, don't worry, Umberto," replied Pupà. "Drink of the water of the Campitelli fountain here, and you will see that your wife will have a child."

Umberto did just that, and shortly afterward it was determined that Agnes was going to have a baby. He always delighted in telling this story. The lack of logic didn't seem to bother him a bit.

Now and then Olivieri would go to the Abruzzi to visit Vincenzino D'Arpizio, Josephine's cousin, with whom he had become friendly. There had been little chance to rebuild after the devastation of the earthquake, with all funds and energies being devoted to the war. The people, however, had begun to rebuild their lives and had returned to the sheep-raising and agriculture which provided their livelihood. Umberto saw the great lake bed of Fùcino, just outside Avezzano, where over sixty square miles of land had been reclaimed in the mid-nineteenth century by Duke Alessandro Torlonia. There were people who said that the draining of the lake had caused the earthquake. The two visited some of the ancient castles of the region, perched on top of pinnacles, causing wonderment as to how they ever could have been built. Vincenzino showed Umberto the treasures he had uncovered at San Benedetto, including gold, silver and bronze coins from the time of the Republic of Rome, extracted from the ancient tombs of the locality. D'Arpizio eventually became well known as an archaeologist and an authority on the antiquities of his area. The two men went for a visit of two days and one night to Pescassèroli, way up in the Apennines. This town is best known as the birthplace of the philosopher Benedetto Croce. At the time of their visit Pescassèroli was an enclave of the past. Life went on as it had for centuries. The people dressed in traditional costumes, woven of native wool. The women wore full skirts and petticoats, beautifully ornamented. It was a real treat.

The Eternal City was spared the destruction of war. Naples gave her a timely warning that Austrian zeppelins were flying to attack her. For several hours the Olivieri family listened to the sounds of the air defense, with some competition from the pounding of their own hearts.

Jessie was born on August 7, 1917, a beautiful baby with golden red hair. She was like a button rose. Umberto and Agnes were sublimely happy. Josephine was thrilled to have a baby sister. Jessie was baptized at the Basilica of Sant'Agnese in the Via Nomentana, built in the fourth century over one of Rome's several catacombs. Isabel da Pozzo was her godmother, a convert from New Zealand, who had married Professor da Pozzo, a painter, and moved to Rome. At the foot of the Spanish Steps, Isabel and her sister opened the Babington Tea Room, known to countless visitors to Rome.

The dreaded war came to an end in November 1918. It had been six long years since Agnes had set eyes on her homeland and her loved ones. By January 1919 the four Olivieris were on their way to America for a visit. They traveled on the first Italian transatlantic steamer released for passenger service. A minesweeper preceded them, just in case. They saw a French liner hit a mine and explode in the ocean. Josephine thought it was another earthquake. Their crossing took twenty-three days, for the ship's captain had deemed it safer to take a more southerly route. Umberto, of course, was seasick most of the time. From previous experience he had developed methods to overcome the terrible malady—medicines to be taken before sailing, rapid walks on the main deck, exercises in deep breathing, meals composed chiefly of anchovies and crackers—but they proved of little avail.

The family remained in the United States slightly over three months. It was the end of the great Spanish flu epidemic. Umberto and Josephine caught it and were hospitalized briefly in Bronxville, New York. Fortunately, their cases were light ones. The

Kents, enchanted with their two granddaughters, reluctantly bade the family farewell. The return trip to Italy was delightful. The Atlantic was peaceful and reflected magnificently the deep blue of the sky. Frequently schools of dolphins danced gracefully on the waves, their sleek, wet coats becoming iridescent in the sunlight. It was almost as if they were happy for the opportunity to entertain the passengers.

Umberto's brother Lello trained to be an *agrimensore,* a surveyor. Carlo entered into a military career as an officer in the cavalry. Young Ottorino distinguished himself in World War I. He was also a cavalry officer, but during the war the cavalry often had to serve in the manner of the infantry. In a battle in the vicinity of Gorizia, Ottorino was in command of a unit of four machine guns. The Austrians destroyed three and killed the soldiers. Ottorino held the position with his single gun and routed an entire Austrian battalion. He was decorated on the battlefield for his bravery, receiving a silver medal from the commander of the Third Army, the duke of Aosta. Once Ottorino was given the honor of opening the court ball by leading the quadrille. Though handsome and dashing, he never married. He was in love with a girl who sold tickets on a street-car, but Mamma Olivieri put her foot down.

The youngest brother, Màssimo, also served in the war. He had to withdraw with his unit at the rout of Caporetto. Shortly afterward he went to live in Brazil with his uncle, a brother of Pietro Olivieri. He married and lived there the rest of his life.

A distant relative became a cherished friend to Umberto and more influential upon his life than some closer family members. Achille Bertini Calosso was the adopted son of a cousin of Umberto's father. The younger men were about the same age and shared an interest in art and literature. Bertini Calosso was, in fact, an expert. He became custodian of medieval monuments in the region of Umbria in central Italy. Umberto later credited his dear friend with giving him his first interest in St. Francis of Assisi.

With his cousin's help Olivieri wrote a monograph on the

Palazzo Venezia in Rome. It was published by Mr. Kent in *Architectural Forum,* one of the leading architectural magazines in New York. The palace was built for Pope Paul II in the fifteenth century, but for over two hundred years it served as the embassy of the Republic of Venice. During the Fascist regime Mussolini lived there, perhaps a manifestation of his desire for imperialism, in that Venice had once been a great maritime empire.

Umberto gathered material for his father-in-law and helped with some of Kent's own publications on Italian architecture. Kent gave his son-in-law a generous acknowledgment in his well-known book on the great sixteenth-century architect Baldassarre Peruzzi.

The lawyer also took an interest in a variety of activities to help reconstruct a torn society. For one, he tried to organize a Boy Scout troop. Josephine remembers that he looked so funny in his short trousers and Scout hat.

He frequently went grouse hunting, accompanied by his favorite bird dog, a large griffon named Nilo. Nilo seemed happy only in the mountains, for he had been born in the Alps and had originally belonged to an Austrian hunter. Sometimes friends would give Olivieri their young bird dogs to train. During the winter he made his own cartridges.

For a while Josephine attended the Grantham School, an exclusive private school for American, English and Austrian girls, but her education was mostly under Umberto's strong direction. His library became her classroom. When able she was taken to places of cultural enrichment. Religion was not stressed.

The war may have been over, but Italy was by no means at peace. Political unrest gave birth to open violence in the streets. Communism threatened to envelop the country. Reaction was swift and strong, the *Fascisti* led by Benito Mussolini. The Kents, reading the daily newspaper accounts in distant New York, became concerned about the safety of their daughter and her family. Mrs. Kent suggested that it might be better if the Olivieris would come to America.

Umberto agreed. He had always wanted to relocate in a new

land of opportunity. The hoped-for appointment to the diplomatic corps had never come. Why not go to America to stay?

Early in 1920 he took a leave of absence from the Treasury Department, at half salary, and returned to the University of Rome to study English. He knew that it would be difficult to pass the bar examination in the United States in order to practice there as an attorney. He would prepare himself to become a teacher. The university granted him a credential to teach English and English literature in the technical institutes and *licei* of the kingdom of Italy. This degree, plus the writing he had done, would serve as his letter of recommendation for a new job in the United States.

Umberto was determined that Josephine should receive her First Holy Communion before the family left Italy. She was sent for a week to the old Cenacle convent, in keeping with family tradition. Umberto's three sisters had prepared there for their First Communion. The convent was in an old palace built without a staircase by an eccentric nobleman who loved horses. He had constructed ramps so that he could ride from room to room and floor to floor. By chance the distinguished Belgian Cardinal Mercier happened to be visiting during Josephine's week of preparation. It was arranged that he should confirm her at the Cenacle. Signora Isabel da Pozzo was her sponsor.

Umberto hired a carriage to take Josephine for a grand tour of Rome. They saw all the historical monuments and all the great churches. From memory he explained their significance in vivid language. They stopped at the Fountain of Trevi to throw in their coins, to be sure that someday each would return to the Eternal City. Josephine was puzzled. Why such a tour? Had she not lived in Rome for over five years? Umberto knew that she had looked without seeing. They ended their farewell visit by eating some delicious sherbet in the beautiful Villa Borghese.

Olivieri had to take his ward to her native town to appear before the municipality. She must make a solemn statement that she wished to remain with her new parents and was willing to leave Italy. This done, he escorted her to the heap of ruins that was once her home. Three or four stairs were unharmed and a piece of the chimney stood erect like a silent sentinel. "This is your land, and this was your house." He spoke with gravity. "This is the place in which you were born and where your father and mother died." He walked away and left her to think the thoughts of an eleven-year-old child.

In November 1920 Umberto Olivieri handed in his resignation to the Treasury Department and prepared to depart Italy with his family for a new life in America. Matilde Santarelli, a dear friend, saw them off. She presented Agnes with a rare volume of prayers, in Latin and Italian, published in Venice in 1758 as a short breviary for use in convents of religious women. Many years later it was to be Umberto's *vade mecum* during his priesthood.

Josephine recalls one special incident of this transatlantic crossing. "One of the passengers came to me as I was lying on a deck chair with the question: 'Little girl, my dear, how many languages do you speak?' Like an insufferable little prig, I answered: 'English, Italian, French.' Suddenly Father's hand rested on my shoulder. He made a bow in the European fashion and said: 'Madam, you will pardon me for speaking, but I must tell you that my daughter is a great disappointment to me. She has not been able to learn any German.' With another bow he excused himself and took me away. The recollection of this episode still makes me feel very small indeed."

The Olivieris remained only a short time in New York. Their first American Christmas was a delight. Josephine was brought to the opera and the museums of the great city, but what she remembers best is the time that Umberto secretly took her to a vaudeville show at the Hippodrome. "He well knew how aghast the rest of the family would be to learn that I had been exposed to such entertainment. There we sat eating popcorn as we watched the magician pull rabbits and eggs out of people's ears. There was a man who ate corn on the cob which rang all sorts of bells as he approached his fingers. The Four Marx Brothers were there, and oh, how Father laughed! That was all well and good until a row of chorus girls in their traditional lack of clothing took the stage. Father became terribly anxious. He told me not to look. The music, the glitter, the audience reaction were too strong a temptation. Father's alarm increased. Suddenly he picked me up and entrusted me to the ministering matron in the ladies' room. When the act was over he came for me."

Olivieri could not find a job. The first school principal to whom he applied was kind enough, at least, to give him a letter of recommendation. How much help it would be was doubtful. The principal noted that "Mr. Olivieri speaks some English." The Kents felt that Umberto might do better in California. It was a young and promising state with only three million people. Mr. Kent had relatives in Berkeley. They would assist Umberto in securing a position. Umberto's spirit of adventure helped to decide quickly in favor of the move, and soon the family of four boarded the Santa Fe train headed for Oakland.

They arrived in the East Bay city on a Saturday. Everything was new and strange. Thoughts of the future were exciting, but also a little frightening. Next day they found a Catholic church and went in for Mass. The priest turned to greet the congregation: "Dominus vobiscum." Umberto Olivieri smiled broadly. "We are at home."

Five

A CALL TO HOLINESS

The Olivieris took rooms at the Harrison Hotel in downtown Oakland, not far from beautiful Lake Merritt. Within a few days Umberto landed his first American job, as a teacher of Spanish in an Oakland high school. It was a good stopgap, at least.

A. P. Giannini founded the Bank of Italy in San Francisco in 1904. He was California born, of Italian descent, and he wanted to start a bank for the "little man," a place where Italian immigrants, especially, could come with confidence to deposit their small savings or to borrow needed capital for their business and agricultural ventures. Giannini succeeded beyond his wildest expectations. By the early twenties the Bank of Italy was well on its way to becoming a statewide system of branch banking. A separate department had been established to deal with the particular problems of Italian investors and depositors, for by that time the bank's appeal had crossed all national and economic lines. Armando Pedrini, a vice-president of the bank, was in charge of the Italian Department.

A cousin of W. W. Kent named Harry May, a prominent governmental lawyer in San Francisco and a resident of Berkeley, went to see Pedrini about a position in the Italian Department for Umberto Olivieri. Pedrini hired him, at a starting salary of $150 a month, to be a legal consultant. Within a few months he was promoted to assistant cashier, much to the annoyance of some of his co-workers with longer service.

In the meantime the Olivieris, with the help of Agnes's parents, had bought a small home on Bancroft Way in Berkeley, close to the University of California. Their antique furniture arrived

Umberto's father, Pietro Olivieri
(*Courtesy Laura Querini*)

Left to right: Costanza, Dino and
Umberto Olivieri in 1888
(*Courtesy Laura Querini*)

Umberto's mother, Teresa Mancini
Olivieri

The Olivieri family spent their summer holidays at Lèvanto on the Italian Riviera. This was about 1900. *Left to right:* Dino, Carlo, Virginia, Umberto, Lello and Costanza. *(Courtesy Laura Querini)*

Umberto's granduncle, Don Raimondo Olivieri of Acqui

In 1903 Umberto enrolled at the University of Rome to study law. *(Courtesy Count Raimondo Olivieri)*

Second Lieutenant Umberto Olivieri at Florence, 1909.
Painted by Arnaldo Tamburini. *(Courtesy de Saisset
Art Gallery, University of Santa Clara)*

Captain Olivieri enjoyed Genoa, 1917. *(Courtesy Sister Josephine Tarquini)*

Fencing was a special thrill for Umberto. He is third from right. *(Courtesy Count Raimondo Olivieri)*

Agnes Kent *(Courtesy Gladys Firpo Floyd)*

Jessie and Josephine, 1918 *(Courtesy Sister Josephine Tarquini)*

Banker Olivieri hoped that he might someday gain a faculty position at the University of California. *(Courtesy Count Raimondo Olivieri)*

When she was old enough Jessie was sent to a private school in California. *(Courtesy Count Raimondo Olivieri)*

Umberto yearned for the outdoors, Yosemite National Park.

The family moved to a larger home on Edgecroft Road in the Berkeley hills. *(Courtesy Gladys Firpo Floyd)*

Umberto became the captain of spiritual retreats for the Italian Catholic Federation. He is at top left.

Professor Umberto Olivieri of
the University of Santa Clara

Umberto and friend on a visit to his daughter and grandchildren.
(Courtesy Gladys Firpo Floyd)

in due time from Rome via the Panama Canal. When the crates were opened, it was discovered that heat had caused expansion of the wood. The inlay had popped out of some of the finest pieces, and the wooden pegs used in lieu of nails had become unglued. Agnes was in tears. Fortunately, after several months in the hands of an expert cabinetmaker, most of the damage was repaired.

The name of Umberto Olivieri soon became known in the Italian-American community of the San Francisco Bay Area. He was involved with Pedrini in the work of the Italian Chamber of Commerce. In 1922 he became secretary of the San Francisco chapter of the Italy-America Society, a cultural group existing also in other parts of the United States. The society had been founded shortly after World War I by Countess Irene di Robilant to foster relations between Italy and the United States. Umberto became a close friend of the noble lady.

At first the family attended Sunday Mass at St. Augustine's parish church on the Oakland-Berkeley line. Then, seeking a more intellectual atmosphere, they began to worship at the Newman Club chapel of the University of California and to take part in the activities of this organization for Catholic students. Agnes went to Mass with the rest of the family, although she never showed any inclination to become a Catholic. Jessie, when she was old enough, was sent to a private school for girls. Josephine, still unable to walk, received an education at home that was equal or superior to anything she might have had at school. Umberto found time to be her principal tutor. He was as demanding of her as his mother had once been of him.

Banker Olivieri hoped that he might someday gain a faculty position on the Berkeley campus. He cultivated the friendship of professors. One was Regis Michaud, who lived near the little house on Bancroft Way. Professor Michaud was a Frenchman, and he loved wine. But those were the days of Prohibition. Umberto managed to come up with a couple of bottles. To show his appreciation Michaud gave him a book on the life of St. Catherine of Siena by Johannes Joergensen, a Danish convert to the Catholic Church. In this devious way God led Umberto Olivieri to the beginning of his great spiritual conversion, a conversion that not only would transform his own life but also would someday bring him into contact with thousands of souls as a priest of Jesus Christ.

The story of his fourteenth-century countrywoman Catherine moved Umberto tremendously. She came of a wealthy family but early in her life chose to live in self-imposed austerity. She was able to bear reverses and trials with sweetness and patience because of the inner serenity that reigned in her soul. After some years of almost total solitude, she entered into an apostolate of charity, wearing the habit of a Dominican tertiary. Soon she attracted a band of followers with whom she humbly shared her wisdom. As her fame spread, she was called upon to mediate political disputes and heal ancient feuds. In this she was eminently successful, for the warring factions found that they could not resist the gentleness of Christ that radiated from this saintly woman. Peace was her noblest cause. Ultimately she became the trusted advisor to two popes and the principal cause of the return of the papacy to Rome from Avignon.

Could it be that Jesus Christ was calling him, Umberto Olivieri, to something more than a routine observance of the rules of religion?

He went back to Professor Michaud. There must be other books. Michaud gave him Joergensen's life of St. Francis of Assisi. Another bottle of wine changed hands. *Il Poverello,* "the little poor man," completely captivated Umberto. To St. Francis, Jesus was a warm, intimate, personal friend. The ragged mendicant from the hills of Umbria was, in fact, so in tune with all of God's creation that he could call the sun and moon, the birds and beasts, his "brothers and sisters" and mean it. He truly loved all men, especially the poor and rejected, with the heart of Christ. Umberto was moved to learn more about St. Francis. He read Chesterton's biography of him. He studied the life by Paul Sabatier, the French Protestant who was largely responsible for a rebirth of interest in St. Francis in the last century.

These books led logically to a careful study of the revolutionary influence of St. Francis on the people of his own time and his continuing impact on Christians and non-Christians down through the ages. Olivieri discovered that there was probably no Catholic saint more acceptable and more meaningful to non-Catholics than Francis of Assisi. He read the lives of Francis's early followers. He traced the history of the Franciscan order. He became fascinated by the life of Father Junípero Serra, the Spanish Franciscan who brought civilization and Christianity to California in the eighteenth century. He made a pilgrimage to the old missions founded by Serra and his successors.

Sometime in 1925 Umberto had to have a tonsillectomy. The surgeon left a piece of tissue which became infected, necessitating a second operation. Even this was not successful, and a delicate third operation was scheduled. Umberto was worried. He went to Holy Mass and recommended himself to the protection of the Blessed Mother. There was no opportunity to go to confession and, since he did not consider himself prepared, he refrained from receiving Holy Communion. While the anesthetic was being administered, he had a sensation of utter darkness. He thought that probably he was dead. He was filled with sorrow that he had not been able to receive Holy Communion. "Blessed Virgin, save me! I don't want to die now!" he prayed. After the operation the doctor told him that his heart had stopped beating momentarily while he was on the table. He was also informed that the abscess, this time removed successfully, had been only three millimeters from one of the major blood vessels.

Reflecting on his close brush with death, Umberto resolved to lead a more dedicated Christian life, to try to be more like St. Francis of Assisi and the others whose lives he had been reading, to share his spiritual insights with his fellowman. The Church, he remembered, prays for the dead: "Let perpetual light shine upon them." His daily prayer became: "Lord, don't let me die in the darkness. Lead me to the light." He meditated over and over again on the first chapter of the Gospel according to St. John. "In him was life, and the life was the light of men. And the light shines in the darkness; and the darkness grasped it not. . . . It was the true light that enlightens every man who comes into the world." (John 1:4-5, 9) In later years Umberto could never quite forgive the Church for eliminating the opening words of St. John's Gospel from their place of honor at the end of every Mass.

Olivieri's work with the Bank of Italy was rather routine—writing letters in Italian for Pedrini and Giannini, dealing with Italian-speaking customers, helping to unsnarl entanglements with the laws of Italy. As he became better known in the San Francisco area, especially through the activities of the Italy-America Society, he was asked to greet and entertain visiting Italian notables. Once General Badoglio came. When he heard, through his aide-de-camp, that Umberto had taken part in the battle of August 15, 1915, on the Carso front, he saw to it that a citation for distinguished service was issued. On another occasion the great Italian aviator De Pinedo paid a visit to San Francisco. Umberto escorted him to City Hall for a reception by the mayor; Agnes rode in a car with Signora de Pinedo. Not long after, an influential Italian-American lady, having read in *Who's Who in America* of the accomplishments of W. W. Kent, arranged a beautiful luncheon with Agnes as the guest of honor.

The elegant social life was only one needed diversion from the daily grind. Umberto yearned for the outdoors. Whenever possible he would go mountain climbing or hunting with friends. He tried deer hunting in Sonoma County, but one look into the eyes of a dying doe was enough. He would stick to quail. The distaff members of the family could tolerate "roughing it" only in a mitigated fashion. He would take them to such places as Yosemite National Park, where they lived in rustic cabins. Such outings, he felt, were especially important for Josephine, who was never allowed to think of herself as "sick" or "crippled." Camp breakfast was invariably a stack of hot pancakes with fresh pork link sausages, an irresistible delicacy for Umberto to the end of his days.

Olivieri invested wisely in Giannini stocks. By 1926 the few hundred dollars of his initial investment had become seven thousand. Once, in a desire to refurbish the office of the Italy-America Society, he risked some of the society's funds in a gamble that the bank's stocks would rise abruptly in the next few days. Luckily, he was right, and the profit realized from the sale of the shares was more than sufficient to purchase the new furniture.

In mid-1926 Umberto and Agnes decided to take a trip to Italy. He wanted to show his parents and family that he had been successful in America and to repay his mother the money she had advanced for his university education. Also, he wanted to visit Assisi to gather more material on St. Francis. He had become inflamed with the desire that San Francisco should honor her patron saint on the seventh centenary of his death. The children were left with friends, and off they went.

On the boat they met a distinguished Mexican family of rice producers and received an open invitation to visit them in Mexico. Umberto's old yearning to see Latin America was re-kindled, but it would be twenty years before he would actually go.

Umberto was glad to see his parents, brothers and sisters again. He told them of his rediscovered spiritual life, and they were a little surprised. At Assisi he had the privilege of meeting Johannes Joergensen, who maintained his home there. The writer encouraged him in his efforts to plan a civic celebration in St. Francis's honor and exhorted him to remain faithful to the spiritual principles of St. Francis. Umberto visited all the places connected with the life of the saint, even the mountain of Alverno where he had received the stigmata. On October 4, 1926, the actual day on which St. Francis died 700 years before, the Olivieris were in London. A beautiful article in an English newspaper convinced Umberto beyond a doubt that when he returned to California he must begin in earnest to lay the groundwork for the celebration.

There were some anxious moments, though, before the Olivieris could leave Italy. Umberto was suspected of anti-Fascist sympathies. Nothing could have been further from the truth. He was, in fact, somewhat favorable toward the Fascist movement because of its relentless opposition to communism, although he was in no way politically active. The suspicion arose from his association with a certain Martinelli in the Italian Chamber of Commerce in San Francisco. Martinelli was a militant anti-Fascist who had been tortured by Mussolini's police. The Olivieris' departure was delayed until the Italian government could be satisfied that Umberto was not involved in any of Martinelli's machinations. A telegram was sent to the Italian Consulate in San Francisco. Agnes was fraught with worry. Would they ever be able to return to the United States? What would happen to the children? Thanks be to God, the consulate soon replied, giving Umberto a clean bill of health.

The family moved to a larger home on Edgecroft Road in the Berkeley hills, with an unobstructed view of San Francisco, the Bay and the Golden Gate. Dinner parties for their wide circle of friends and for distinguished visitors became more frequent. Umberto always prepared the dinner. Josephine remembers it well:

"Father would go to his office in the morning and return after lunch, at which time he vigorously took possession of the kitchen. What an afternoon! I was kept busy chopping this and peeling that. Kaya, our trusted Japanese helper, had her elbows constantly in soapsuds in her effort to keep chaos out of her domain. A utensil was never used twice by Father. All supplies and condiments had to be kept within sight and reach, and woe to anyone who tried to put some semblance of order to the kitchen while he was holding forth! He would fire questions in rapid succession to me asking what he should add next as the *Risotto alla Milanese* was being slowly stirred or as the *Pollo alla Livornese* was fragrantly sizzling in the frying pan. I glowed with satisfaction if I answered correctly. When the seven-course dinner in the making could be safely entrusted to others, Father, completely exhausted, would rest, take a bath and become his charming self in a tuxedo, ready to be a host. It delighted him no end to hear the guests compliment him upon having such a chef.

"He had a beautiful Italian tenor voice. All loved to hear

him sing the arias from the operas or the old favorites like 'O Sole Mio' and 'Santa Lucia Lontana.' In addition to the quality of his voice and range of notes, he was able to supply the needed dramatic modulations. The expression on his face and the use of his hands and arms conveyed perfectly the meaning of the Italian words. He was in constant demand, but I am sure that he had no more ardent admirer than myself. I did not permit myself to go to sleep until I had heard him sing. From my bed I joined the guests in appreciative hand clapping."

Olivieri enjoyed arranging social and cultural events for the members and guests of the Italy-America Society. One particularly successful evening was held in the splendid Crocker mansion in San Mateo, home of one of San Francisco's most prominent banking families. Umberto persuaded the Italian operatic tenor Tito Schipa to entertain at the festivities. He sang beautifully. The guests at the reception were completely enchanted.

On another occasion Schipa was singing *Manon* in San Francisco. Umberto and Agnes were in the orchestra in formal dress. At the end of the aria called "The Dream" Umberto stood up and rang out with a vibrant *"Viva, Tito Schipa! Viva!"* The opera house picked up his vivas while he ran backstage and threw his arms around the tenor.

Umberto Olivieri was much in demand as a contributor to Italian-American publications and as a lecturer on Italian art and culture. There was no objection from A. P. Giannini, of course, because all of this was excellent free advertising for the Bank of Italy. Umberto became more and more preoccupied with such activities, especially as the time for the civic celebration in honor of St. Francis drew nearer. Often he would work far into the night researching and preparing his articles and lectures. He had learned to get along with only four or five hours' sleep, taking catnaps during the day when needed. New interests were always competing for his time. The subject of the Protestant Reformation caught his attention and he studied it in depth. He felt honored whenever asked to be a guest speaker at the renowned University of California. One lecture on the works of

Giotto in the Basilica of St. Francis in Assisi was especially well received.

Preparation for the St. Francis celebration required many months of arduous effort. First, the civil and ecclesiastical authorities had to be convinced that such a celebration was desirable and feasible. Then, the citizenry of San Francisco and the Bay Area had to be stirred to an enthusiastic response. Endorsements were sought and received from scholars and churchmen. Olivieri went to see Mr. F. Gordon O'Neill, manager and editor of *The Monitor,* weekly publication of the Archdiocese of San Francisco. His reaction was less than heartening. Only with difficulty did Umberto finally persuade him to give the event the needed publicity among the Catholic people. Advertising agencies also cooperated by donating billboard space on the streetcars.

Early in his campaign Olivieri secured the active support of Dr. Frederick W. Clampett, a retired Protestant minister, well known in San Francisco for his newspaper column. Dr. Clampett was a great admirer of St. Francis. The two men worked together to form a citizens' committee representative of all faiths and nationalities. Initial efforts had been under the aegis of the Italy-America Society. Financial support was solicited from bankers and merchants.

The Franciscans, of course, would have to be involved. Umberto went to St. Elizabeth's Friary in East Oakland to enlist their participation. Clampett inaugurated an essay contest for high-school students on the subject "St. Francis of Assisi, Lover of Men." Ten cash prizes, aggregating $510, were donated.

Umberto took a personal hand in arranging the program. Many times he had witnessed assemblies at the Palazzo della Cancellerìa in Rome. He wanted this celebration to have something of the same elegance.

The festivities were set for the evening of Tuesday, November 22, 1927, in the huge civic auditorium of San Francisco. There was to be no admission charge. Last-minute publicity, including several newspaper editorials, urged attendance. Umberto and his co-workers were not disappointed. Over eight thousand men, women, and children filled the auditorium almost to capacity. For three hours the throng was "held by the exquisite music and the elegant speeches."

The principal address was delivered by Brother Leo of St. Mary's College, located at that time in Oakland. Brother Leo was an author and public speaker known and respected throughout the United States by people of all faiths and no faith, much as Bishop Fulton J. Sheen was to be revered a generation later. A member of the Brothers of the Christian Schools, Brother Leo was a dear personal friend of the Olivieris and a frequent guest in their home. Agnes was always happy to have this interesting conversationalist at her table. Later, unfortunately, his popularity waned when he was dispensed from his religious vows and left his order to marry.

"San Francisco and Assisi," spoke Brother Leo, "are two cities different in external aspect but united by a common bond. Perhaps more people have heard of little Assisi than of great San Francisco. Our fame is largely in the future and rests in our many hands to make. Assisi's fame rests in one personality, in the accomplishments of one man. Assisi, not rich, nor tall-towered, its schools modest, no trolley cars, no football teams, lives enshrined in the heart of the world.

"To understand Francis we must remember the general truth that the life of man is shaped by philosophy. There are two great philosophies. One is of the man who knows that fire burns, rain wets, money is needed for comfort, sustenance is required at certain periods of the day. Eat, drink and save money for tomorrow is at best uncertain. The man of the other philosophy commits the unpardonable sin of making people think. He forgets meals and has no money in the bank; he is trying on his family if he has one; he is animated by one great idea. He may be a musician, a poet, an artist or a saint. These, when real musicians, poets, artists, saints, though different in many ways, have this in common, that they take little heed of food, clothing, and all the externals the rest of us think most of the time about. 'After all these things do the heathens seek.'

"We can best understand Francis, as Dante did, if we realize that he was once a wealthy man who, having heard of a pearl of great price, gave up all to find it. He lived for the best that life affords and wanted to share his find with others. He sought to restore the greater gifts of God to man. For this one great purpose he stripped himself of worldly cares as an athlete strips for the contest.

"Even as the Statue of Liberty stands in New York harbor, I would like to see on one of our proud hills at this western gate a statue of 'the little poor man of Assisi,' a statue of the great lover to bring hope and life to troubled hearts, a statue with garments careless enough, girt with a cord, and the two arms extended—St. Francis loving the world."

Francis's disciples in their brown robes mingled with the crowd and distributed programs. They displayed a beautiful simplicity that won people's hearts in the manner of their founder. The souvenir program contained three poems in honor of St. Francis written for the occasion by Ina Coolbrith, Edwin Markham and Nancy Buckley.

On either side of the massive auditorium organ was a heroic painting of St. Francis, one showing him as a humble friar, robed, corded and barefoot, the other as a heavenly saint, hands raised in benediction. The stage was decorated in evergreens. A choir of thirty-two Franciscans from Oakland and Santa Barbara opened and closed the evening's program with soulful Gregorian chant.

Former U.S. Sen. James D. Phelan made introductory remarks and read a cable of congratulation from Premier Mussolini. Mayor James Rolph, Jr., extended the greetings of the city of San Francisco. Other speakers were Dean Paul F. Cadman of the University of California and the Right Reverend Edward L. Parsons, Episcopal bishop of California. Dean Cadman paid tribute to the humility and courtesy of St. Francis: "His humility is to us an allegory, for we would not give away our cloak. Yet through the din and roar and hurry of our civilization that demands more and more luxuries comes his voice asking us, 'What shall it profit a nation if it gains the whole world and loses its soul?' His spirit of kindliness and courtesy teaches us the rare attribute that 'manners maketh the man.' And the widely known courteous and hospitable atmosphere of San Francisco perchance is the benediction of the spirit of St. Francis."

The San Francisco Symphony Orchestra under the baton of Alfred Hertz rendered Liszt's "Les Preludes" and a tone poem by Herman Hans Wetzler recalling St. Francis's love of birds. The 400-voice San Francisco Municipal Chorus, directed by Hans Leschke, performed the Lateran Chorus from Wagner's *Rienzi* and the Sanctus from Verdi's *Manzoni Requiem*.

Dr. Clampett announced the winners of the essay contest. He summoned Umberto Olivieri to the stage to receive the crowd's acclaim, but the originator of the celebration, in the spirit of Franciscan simplicity, managed to remain at his seat to acknowledge the applause.

The Most Reverend Edward J. Hanna, archbishop of San Francisco, gave the closing prayer, one attributed to St. Francis: "May God have mercy upon us and keep us. May He make His face to shine upon us and grant us peace."

The following day the newspapers printed glowing reports. Umberto's name was not mentioned. O'Neill of *The Monitor* knew the part he had played, however, and when the weekly next appeared wrote as follows: "The city is indebted to Umberto Olivieri for having conceived it, enlisted the support of able men and women, and carried it out with such exquisite taste. Chesterton has said that if Francis, the very poor and humble man, retained one luxury it was the manners of a court. Olivieri and his associates made of this celebration a court reception in honor of St. Francis. . . . Men who have been attending public functions in San Francisco for many years told the writer that this was the most refined public affair held in San Francisco in twenty years."

A few days after the celebration Archbishop Hanna sent Umberto a letter of thanks: "Rarely has any great demonstration brought me the joy that I experienced the other night at the Auditorium. The crowd was even beyond my expectation and the quality of the entertainment was so fine, that I can hardly find words to tell you my appreciation. To you above everyone else, the credit for the success is due." Unfortunately, he did not advert specifically to the subject of the celebration in the text of his letter, rendering the letter less useful as a reference for Umberto in future years. For the remainder of his life, though, Umberto Olivieri considered the civic celebration of the seventh centenary of the death of St. Francis of Assisi his most satisfying accomplishment as a layman.

The joy of the successful celebration soon gave way to sadness for Umberto when he received the news of the death of his brother Ottorino in Rome. A brain tumor had ended the life of the plucky soldier at thirty-two. Pietro Olivieri wrote, "This great sorrow that is falling on us now I feel is going to shorten my old age." His words proved true, for he was dead the following July.

It was only two days after the glorious tribute to St. Francis that the front pages of the San Francisco newspapers were filled with the news of the martyrdom of Father Miguel Pro in Mexico. Umberto was seized by a desire to go to Mexico to fight with the *Cristeros,* an underground guerilla movement working to restore the rights of the Church. He went to ask advice of the priest at the Newman Club. The wise pastor quickly dissuaded him. "You have a wife and two children to support. Your duty is to stay with them."

Encouraged by the triumphant celebration in honor of St. Francis, Olivieri began another project: to establish a Chair of Italian Culture at the University of California. He wrote to Papini and other outstanding Italian men of letters for their endorsements. He contacted eminent professors of the University of Rome. With Armando Pedrini he approached A. P. Giannini for an endowment. He traveled up and down California collecting other funds. Finally, in 1929, he had the great joy of introducing Professor Carlo Formichi, the distinguished professor of English literature and of Sanskrit at the University of Rome, as the first incumbent of the Chair. In recognition of Umberto's efforts in this cause and so many others, the Italian government presented him with a bronze medal of merit for the promotion of Italian culture outside of Italy.

Agnes and Umberto Olivieri separated in March 1929. It would serve no purpose here to recount the details—most of which we do not know—of the disintegration of a once-happy marriage. It suffices to remember that, as it takes two to make a marriage, it likewise takes two to break one. There was an unpleasant divorce. Custody of Jessie was awarded to Agnes. Josephine, who, contrary to all medical expectations, was now able to walk without too much difficulty, went to Boston to learn to be a social worker. Umberto was left alone.

Many years of bitter loneliness would pass before Umberto Olivieri could come to accept the tragedy of the failure of his marriage as being somehow part of God's plan that he should serve Him as a priest.

Six

TEACHER OF
HIS FELLOWMAN

Umberto Olivieri, at the age of forty-five, set about to re-build his shattered life. Remarriage for him, a committed Catholic, was out of the question. He considered himself bound by the ties of his marriage as long as both he and his wife should live. He remembered the sage advice given him so many years before by Father Antonino of the Trinitarians of San Carlino. With God's help he would be able to bear his cross.

More and more Umberto devoted himself to the lay apostolate of Catholic Action. He traveled to many places in California and Nevada under the auspices of the Italian Catholic Federation, an organization founded in San Francisco by Luigi Providenza to call Italian Catholics to a more fervent practice of their religion. Umberto lectured, taught catechism, tried to inspire "fallen-aways" to return to the sacraments. One of his favorite and most successful endeavors was among the large Italian community in the high desert town of Yerington, Nevada. He returned there often.

He became the captain of spiritual retreats for the Italian Catholic Federation. His frequent retreats at El Retiro, the Jesuit retreat house in Los Altos, California, introduced him to the spirituality of St. Ignatius of Loyola and inspired him to set aside a daily period for meditation. The life of the Spanish soldier appealed to him. With St. Ignatius he would pray daily: "Take, O Lord, and receive all my liberty, my memory, my understanding, and my entire will, all that I have and possess.

Thou hast given all to me; to Thee, O Lord, I return it. All is Thine; dispose of it according to Thy will. Give me Thy love and Thy grace, for this is enough for me."

Umberto, having given up his home and taken a room at the Professors' Club in Berkeley, became a frequent dinner guest of East Bay leaders of the I.C.F. Mrs. Gina Griffanti, at that time much involved with the I.C.F. branch in El Cerrito's St. John the Baptist parish, remembers the first time that Mr. Olivieri came to her home—uninvited! He phoned one afternoon and announced that he would be there for dinner that evening. She did not know who he was! Her husband, Joe, now deceased, who had met Umberto casually, reassured her that he was an important figure in the I.C.F. and a worthy dinner guest. His charming manners and conversation redeemed his boldness, and they became fast friends.

Another lasting friendship was made with Father John B. Savio. This Italian-born priest, not quite a year Umberto's junior, was pastor of St. Michael's, a rural parish near Stockton, California. He had once been a member of the Consolata, an Italian missionary order, and had served in Africa. He had also seen distinguished service as a combat soldier in World War I, even though he was already a priest at the time. The bravery of those earlier days and the simplicity with which he was now living in that poor country parish impressed Umberto very much. He traveled frequently to Stockton to draw inspiration from Father Savio.

Olivieri's net worth at its greatest amounted to some $90,000, most of it in stocks of the Giannini banking interests. The stocks took a nose dive in 1928, recovered, then plummeted again in the nationwide stock market crash of October 1929, the beginning of the Great Depression. By the terms of the divorce action Agnes received half the couple's assets, including their lovely home. Umberto was never reduced to destitution, but he had to settle for a manifestly simpler way of life than that to which he had become accustomed. He adjusted with a minimum of difficulty. Material things simply were not that important to him now. Though he did not realize it at the time, God was purging him, by stages, of all worldly and even family attachments so as to prepare him to give himself completely to others in priestly service.

In his experiences as a banker Umberto saw many examples of the futility of amassing earthly riches. One story he would tell in later years concerns an immigrant Italian barber who had a small shop on Union Street in San Francisco. Giannini had helped him to get started in business. The barber invested a small sum in the stocks of the young Bank of Italy and realized a handsome profit. Soon he was overcome by avarice. He put his shop in the hands of an employee and devoted his entire attention to speculation on the stock exchange. Over the years he became a multimillionaire. He bought property in Italy and on Nob Hill in San Francisco. He gave lavish presents to the members of his family. Even with the decline of the market he managed to salvage a million dollars or more. But, with all his wealth, he was an unhappy man. One of his children died at the age of twelve. The older children, well educated in San Francisco, were ashamed of their unlettered father's broken English. When they brought their friends home they suggested, not too subtly, that "Papà should pay a visit to his old barber shop." One day he went to the shop and spent some time in conversation with the man who was taking care of his customers. Finally, he told the assistant barber to go home for the day. "I'll lock up for you," he said. He wrote a brief note: "I was happier when I worked in this little shop than I am as a millionaire." There was a stove where the curling iron could be heated or water boiled for shaving. He opened the gas jet. His body was found the next morning.

The depreciation of the Giannini stocks unnerved depositors and investors. Letters, some in Italian, poured in to the bank. Olivieri had the job of answering those in his native language and assuring the worried customers that the management of the bank was sound and their money was safe. One such letter, he remembered, had to be written to a priest. The priest had sent a bitter complaint, full of violent and abusive language. Umberto replied as kindly as possible that the writer had every right to register his grievance, but that his letter was far from being worthy of a priest. "Remember the words of St. Augustine: *'In necessariis unitas, in dubiis libertas, sed in omnibus caritas!'* " (In essentials, unity; in doubtful matters, freedom; but in all things, charity!)

One time Umberto was sent by the bank's Italian Department to visit personally the well-to-do Italians of Reno, Nevada, to restore their confidence in the bank, at that time beset by internal difficulties. On Sunday morning he went to the adjoining small railroad town of Sparks, intending to call upon some of the people there whose names he had been given. But first, he must go to Mass. He spotted a nicely dressed man walking down the street with three children, two girls and a little boy. He asked directions to the nearest Catholic church. The gentleman replied, "It is just over there a few blocks, but we are going there, too. You can come with us if you like." Umberto gladly accepted the invitation and was delighted to be asked to their home for breakfast afterward. This was the beginning of an important friendship.The man, Lewis LaVoy, a French-Canadian, worked for the Southern Pacific Railroad. His wife was a convert to the Catholic faith. Umberto visited them often over the years and watched their eight children grow to maturity. The two girls he had first met with their father on the way to church are now Sister Ignatius and Sister Gerald of the Dominican Sisters of San Rafael. The little boy entered the seminary, took his theology at North American College in Rome, and is now Father Elwood LaVoy of the Diocese of Reno.

It was about this time that Umberto Olivieri decided to become an American citizen. His future, whatever it might be, lay here in the United States. Or so he thought.

Meanwhile, Josephine did well in her social-service studies in Boston. Her father left her completely independent, as she wished, and she managed to get by on a tight budget. Her field work brought her into contact with poor immigrants living in the rickety tenements of Boston's Italian ghetto. Up and down the stairs she climbed. Her legs gave her increasing difficulty, and her field supervisor became alarmed. Finally she was told that she could not return to work without a doctor's approval. She had saved enough to pay the orthopedist but could not afford the required X ray. Promptly she sent her father a collect telegram: "Need $25. Hip X ray." His answer came with equal promptitude, also collect: "Whose hip is it?" He had not forgotten how his father had treated him when he was a young lieutenant in Florence. Now Josephine, like himself, had to find someone with a kinder purse and would have to carry the heavy burden of debt for many a day.

Upon completion of her studies Josephine returned to San Francisco and obtained a position as a social worker with the Italian Board of Relief. One day a young mother abandoned an illegitimate baby in her office. She drove the baby to St. Elizabeth's Infant Shelter, operated by the Daughters of Charity of St. Vincent de Paul. One of the sisters answered the door and received the infant with open arms and a smile that came from a heart filled with love. That smile was a turning point in Josephine's life. Imagine Umberto's joy when, in 1932, he learned that his foster daughter had entered the Daughters of Charity. For this, he knew now, God had led him to earthquake-stricken Avezzano in 1915.

A. P. Giannini, in an effort to extend his banking operations nationwide, had allowed himself to lose control of the Bank of Italy, by then known as Bank of America. New York bankers, jealous of Giannini's successes, had contrived to insinuate themselves into the top management of the bank. They had won over to their way of thinking some of Giannini's most trusted aides. Now, from Giannini's viewpoint, they threatened to destroy all that he had stood and worked for since 1904. He resolved to regain the upper hand. There was a heated proxy battle. The vast majority of the stockholders stood by him, and Giannini won handily. He could not allow those who had gone against him to remain with the bank. So, early in 1932, out went James A. Bacigalupi, once president of the bank. Out went Armando Pedrini, who had been with Giannini from the very beginning. And out went Umberto Olivieri.

Bacigalupi had a brother, Father Eugene Bacigalupi, S.J., on the faculty of the University of Santa Clara. Through his efforts, principally, Umberto secured a teaching position at the Jesuit institution in September 1932. His education at the University of Rome and his distinguished career as a writer and lecturer were superlative credentials. Sylvester Andriano, a prominent San Francisco attorney, put in a good word for him. Professor Rudolph Altrocchi, chairman of the department of Italian at the University of California, gave him an enviable recommendation. Santa Clara's professor of Italian had taken a leave of absence. Olivieri was assigned to his classes.

The Italian classes met three times a week. Most of the students enrolled were of Italian descent. In those days Santa Clara was a boys' school of only a few hundred students. Classes in Italian were understandably small. The first year, elementary Italian, stressed grammar, pronunciation, vocabulary, syntax and reading from simpler prose. The second, or intermediate, year moved into more difficult translation, oral and written exercises, and more advanced reading. Predictably, only about half of the first-year students continued into the second year. The third year, Italian literature, concentrated on Dante. At times there were only three or four students in the advanced class, some years only one.

David Arata, presently and for many years registrar of the University of Santa Clara, was one of Professor Olivieri's students in the early thirties. They became lifelong friends. He remembers that Olivieri conducted every class, if there were at least two students, in the same formal classroom manner. He paced back and forth while lecturing. The boys used to make a game of counting the number of times he would cross a certain crack in the floor during the class period. In the smaller classes, if you were not prepared, it was better to cut the class, for you were sure to be called upon at least twice. A Dante class with only one student was taught in the professor's office.

Many of Professor Olivieri's "boys" went on to achieve prominence in law, education and medicine. There are superior court judges and superintendents of schools in California who once sat at his feet. In 1936 a year of elementary French was added to the professor's schedule. One of his French students in 1940-41 was Paul Laxalt, later governor of Nevada and at this writing a U.S. senator from the Silver State.

Umberto became moderator of the Nobili Club, a campus society for students of Italian, named for the founder of the university. (After 1949 membership was open to all foreign-language students.) Once or twice a semester the club would gather for an Italian-style banquet with a guest speaker. The Italian consul came several times. Professor Olivieri invariably broke into song during or after the banquet. The students loved to hear him. It was almost like the days of the fancy dinner parties on Edgecroft Road in the Berkeley hills. The Nobili Club banquets were usually held at a local restaurant, sometimes the old Torino Hotel in San Jose. On occasion they would go to the home of one of the students. Dave Arata gave a barbecue once at his family's ranch. During the depression the day students—Santa Clara was both boarding and day school—were asked to bring a gallon of homemade wine apiece.

For exercise Professor Olivieri loved to go climbing on nearby Mount Hamilton. He would often take a few of his students, usually from among the boarders, with him on these jaunts. They had difficulty in keeping up with him.

He cut a striking figure on the Santa Clara campus, tall, slightly balding, with neatly trimmed mustache, nattily dressed, never without a tie, pocket handkerchief always in place. The students nicknamed him "Professor C. Aubrey Smith" after a movie actor who took the part of English sophisticates. Once Umberto traveled to Chicago to visit Sister Josephine. He was met at the station by his foster daughter and her companion, Sister Helen. He stepped from the train elegantly dressed in a dark brown pair of trousers, a tweed coat, a brown hat, with a lovely brown leather camera case swinging from his shoulder. Sister Helen exclaimed, "Oh, your father is an Englishman!" Being every inch an Englishwoman herself that was the highest compliment she could pay him.

In April 1933 Umberto received the sad news of the death

of his mother. He wished that they had had a closer relationship, but he was grateful for her strict discipline that had helped him to lead a successful life. He promised to pray for her soul daily.

For the first couple of years he lived on campus in one of the residence halls. Later he bought a small house on Lafayette Street close to the university. He attended Mass and received Holy Communion every day. Soon after his arrival at Santa Clara he participated in reviving San Jose's Sacred Heart Fraternity of the Third Order of St. Francis, becoming a tertiary himself and following the daily rule faithfully. He also joined the Knights of Columbus.

Beginning in 1932 he served for about eight years as editor of *L'Unione,* a Catholic weekly newspaper in Italian published by the Archdiocese of San Francisco. In this position he worked closely with the Salesian Fathers of Don Bosco. He also contributed articles to *La Voce del Pòpolo,* a San Francisco Italian-language daily, to the *Giornale d'Italia* of Rome, and to other periodicals. His schedule of lectures to clubs, cultural groups and schools continued unabated. Among his subjects were the relationship of Church and State, the encyclicals of Pius XI and Pius XII, fascism, communism, the League of Nations, and the political theories of Dante.

In 1937 the Spanish National Committee of San Francisco published a pamphlet by Olivieri entitled *Democracy! Which Brand, Stalin's or Jefferson's?* He also delivered a stirring lecture in defense of Franco, attended by more than five hundred persons at the Hotel Excelsior in San Francisco. He was introduced as the "distinguished *catedrático italiano* of Santa Clara." Not long afterward a wealthy Spanish widow gave a lovely dinner party in his honor. It soon became apparent to Umberto that she was looking for a proposal of marriage, so he quickly terminated the friendship.

Father Savio was transferred to Holy Cross Church in San Jose in 1937. This is an Italian national parish. Olivieri often took his evening meal at the rectory. Father Savio gave him odd jobs to do—taking parish census, helping the poor and the sick, driving visiting bishops and priests, etc. He enjoyed being associated with the priestly ministry. Soon he became a familiar figure to the parishioners. Once he had to drive a priest to visit Father Savio who was hospitalized in Oakland. They arrived around noontime, and the nursing sister offered to bring them a little lunch to eat by Father Savio's bedside. At that moment, unfortunately, a Holy Cross parishioner who had taken a dislike to Umberto walked in. Soon it was all over the parish that "Olivieri was ordering steak" to be billed to the parish account. For the most part, though, his presence and activity in the parish were welcome.

The parents of some of his students would ask him to dinner now and then. There was always a place for him at the Giovannonis' table. Umberto would announce himself by singing an Italian aria with improvised words: "No one, but absolutely no one, could concoct such a delectable dish from which emanates a fragrance that cannot be matched anywhere!" His hostess was left speechless and breathless.

One of Professor Olivieri's favorite spots was the cloistered Carmelite Monastery in Santa Clara, with its striking Spanish Renaissance church and tower and its cool, shaded gardens. He admired Father Shepherd, an elderly Jesuit, who walked there daily, half a mile or more, to celebrate Mass. Umberto loved to sing the High Masses and Benedictions for the Carmelite Sisters. Sister Gertrude, the "outside Sister," became a close friend and spiritual guide. Eventually he came to know Mother Agnes of Jesus, the prioress. The monastery had been built by her wealthy family a few years after she took the veil as a young woman. Senator James D. Phelan was her uncle. Frequently Umberto would visit with Mother Agnes through the grille. Her wisdom and insight enlightened him and her understanding heart sustained him in times of discouragement.

Professor Olivieri made many friends among the Jesuit staff at Santa Clara, from Father Gianera, the president of the University, to a humble Jesuit lay brother. This little old Frenchman, who could not read, impressed Umberto by his piety. His "prayerbook" consisted of holy cards and religious pictures. Then there were Father Boland, the librarian; Father Fagothey, the ethics professor; and Father Deeney, to whom Umberto frequently went for spiritual advice. Among the lay professors he enjoyed the company of Martin Glavina, the German teacher; Carlo Flumiani, a fellow Italian who taught economics and political science; and Victor Vari, a young Italian professor of languages whom Olivieri regarded as a protégé.

For a while Jessie came to live with her father in the little house on Lafayette Street. Many of the Santa Clara "Broncos" would have loved to date the red-haired beauty, but Papà was very protective in the European manner and succeeded in frightening them away. He sent Jessie to Europe for a year to study Italian culture at the University of Bologna. She had the joy of meeting her Italian family, really for the first time, because she was only three years old when her parents left Italy. Jessie, like Josephine, was placed on a strict budget, but she was having such a good time that the budget was soon forgotten. One day she and a friend decided to go to Paris for the holidays. She promptly cabled her father, collect: "To Paris. Need money." His answer came back immediately, collect: "Go Paris. No money." To Paris she did go, but all that she could afford to eat in the city of *haute cuisine par excellence* was coffee and brioche.

Jessie married Ignatius (Nace) Firpo, of an Oakland Italian family, at the Cathedral of St. Thomas Aquinas in Reno in 1940. Umberto sang Arcadelt's "Ave Maria" at their wedding. They went to make their home at gorgeous Lake Tahoe. Umberto looked forward to visiting them on weekends. They presented him with three lovely grandchildren, Johnny, Steffie and Vickie.

It was in 1941 that Father Bernardino Banci, a Franciscan friar, came from Italy to California to preach a mission for the Italian Catholic Federation. Umberto had been giving a great deal of thought to the possibility of entering religious life. He was not sure that he would be accepted, on account of his age and his status as a divorced man, and for those reasons he had practically ruled out the priesthood. In a conversation with Father Banci he mentioned his hopes and misgivings. The Italian priest told him that, if he could find a bishop to sponsor

him, it was possible for him to receive a papal dispensation to
be ordained.

This was heartening news! In the next few years Professor
Olivieri made several inquiries and applications. He did not
consider the Jesuits, for their years of preparation are unusually
long and difficult. Oddly, he who was such an admirer of St.
Francis and a member of the Third Order did not apply to the
Franciscans. Many years earlier Father Antonino of San Carlino
had advised him against entering the Franciscan Order because
he did not consider him suited to the life, with long hours each
day to be spent in choir. It is also possible that, at this later
point in his life, Umberto was so overwhelmed by St. Francis
and the Franciscan heritage that he did not consider himself
worthy to be other than a third-rank member. Nevertheless,
he did apply to enter the Trappists, a cloistered order much
stricter than the Franciscans and with many more hours of choir.
The Abbot of Huntsville, Utah, replied kindly that he did not
think Umberto would be able to stand the rigors of the life.

Olivieri asked Father Savio to speak to Archbishop John J.
Mitty of San Francisco in his behalf. His application was re-
jected immediately—"too old." He wrote to Bishop Charles F.
Buddy of San Diego, well known for his kindness and leniency.
The answer was that, in his opinion, Umberto "does not have a
vocation." Once Umberto happened to meet Bishop Robert J.
Armstrong of Sacramento at the home of their mutual friends,
the Cristofanis, at McCloud near Mount Shasta. He told Bishop
Armstrong of his desires. The bishop laughed. It became clear to
Umberto Olivieri that it would take a major miracle for him
to become a priest or religious. Probably the best he could hope
for would be that some monastery or religious house take him in
residence as a layman, without vows, and allow him to live the
life of the community as much as possible under the circumstances.

In 1941 Professor Olivieri taught Italian to members of the
United States Army going overseas, a special course at Stanford
University. There were times during World War II that the
University of Santa Clara closed down certain departments for

lack of students. Umberto was laid off. For a while he worked in a shipyard, then in a munitions factory. He came home exhausted every day. Physical work was a change for him and taught him respect for the laboring man. At a time when anti-Italian sentiments ran high, he was denounced to the president of Santa Clara University. Father Gianera knew, of course, that he was a loyal American, and the complaints came to naught. Toward the end of the war he went one day to visit some Italian prisoners of war interned in California, hoping to cheer them up a bit by bringing them some reading material in Italian. He made a few remarks that might have been considered critical of the American way of life and was promptly silenced by a United States Army officer who overheard him and understood Italian.

Shortly after the war Umberto worked briefly for Caritas Dei, a charitable organization that sent relief parcels to Italy. He accepted a small salary for his work—he had no other employment at the time since the university had not yet resumed full activity—although others volunteered their services. The program was under the direction of his old friend Sylvester Andriano, a lawyer who worked closely with the Italian Consulate. The packages contained flour, sugar, medicine, etc. Each parcel was valued at about five dollars. The office of Caritas Dei was located in North Beach, a traditionally Italian section of San Francisco. In order to get to his work Umberto had to cross through the park in front of the large Salesian Church of Sts. Peter and Paul. There, daily, he saw Italian men of sixty-five or seventy years of age sitting on the benches, reading the newspaper, smoking their pipes, even sleeping. Umberto reflected that he was now over sixty years old. "My goodness!" he said to himself, "I don't want to get to that point! I don't want to be one of those men with nothing to do!"

Umberto Olivieri made his first trip to Mexico in the summer of 1946. The first month he stayed in Guadalajara, practicing his Spanish in what was then a much smaller city. He had the opportunity to meet many interesting people. He did, of course, travel to Querétaro to fulfill his boyhood promise to see the place where Emperor Maximilian had been executed. He toured the

Franciscan monastery where his hero had been held prisoner.
At Querétaro Umberto was less than a hundred miles from the
Valley of the Mezquital, but at that time he had not even heard
of the place. He visited Mexico City and the Basilica of Our Lady
of Guadalupe. He saw Puebla and other charming cities. From
Taxco he wrote: "Dear Jessie and Nace: This is the climax
of my trip. This is the most lovely spot on this part of America.
Landscape, houses, churches, gardens are just ideal. I hope we
can all come here together."

While continuing at Santa Clara Professor Olivieri took a
second position as a teacher of Spanish at Stanford during the
academic year 1946-47. His beloved daughter Jessie died un-
expectedly of postoperative complications in March 1947. She
had not reached her thirtieth birthday. Her husband was left
with three tiny children to rear. Umberto was heartbroken. He
plunged himself deeper and deeper into his work to try to escape
the pain of his loss.

God had now left him completely alone and entirely free.
His wife was gone. His home was gone. His wealth was gone.
Josephine was faraway in a convent. Jessie, too, was taken from
him. It would be easier now to hear the gentle whisper of the
Holy Spirit calling him to something new and wonderful. And
that call would not be long in coming.

The famous Father Riccardo Lombardi, S.J., founder of
the Movement for a Better World, came to give a series of
lectures in California on the occasion of the twenty-fifth anniver-
sary of the founding of the Italian Catholic Federation. Professor
Olivieri was privileged to accompany him and serve as his
interpreter. Santa Clara allowed Olivieri to take a few weeks off
to go with Father Lombardi to Chicago and on to New York,
from where he returned to Italy.

Umberto also had the opportunity to help Father John M. De
Marchi, an author and authority on Our Lady of Fatima. This priest
of the Consolata Order came to California to visit the Portuguese
communities and gather money for the Consolata's mission at
Fatima. He asked Father Savio's assistance. The pastor, in turn,
requested Professor Olivieri to see to the comfort and convenience

of Father De Marchi. Every night for several weeks Umberto drove him to this or that California city or town. They became good friends. When the tour was completed, Father De Marchi, as a gesture of appreciation, offered Father Savio a trip to Fatima. "No," the pastor replied, "I cannot leave my parish, but if it's all right with you I'll send Professor Olivieri."

The trip to Europe in the summer and early autumn of 1948 was Umberto's first since 1926. He stayed forty days at Fatima, living in the simple accommodations of the Consolata house. The rough bed in which he slept, he was edified to learn, had recently been occupied by the Count of Paris, pretender to the throne of France, who had made a pious pilgrimage to Fatima. Umberto spent thrilling days walking here and there to the sites made famous by Our Lady's appearances to three Portuguese children in 1917. He went to Aljustrel to meet the parents of Francisco and Jacinta and was invited to share their humble supper. The aging couple gave him precious relics of the two dead children's clothing. In all, the events of three decades earlier became very real to Umberto through his association with the people and the places that had witnessed them. He was sure that it would be to just such poor and simple folk as these that the Blessed Virgin would choose to manifest herself, and through them to the world.

One day, at the procession of the Blessed Sacrament, he saw a miracle with his own eyes. A crippled nun, lying flat on a stretcher, arose and stood erect as she was blessed by her Eucharistic Lord. Umberto learned the circumstances of her illness and satisfied himself beyond doubt that this was a genuine cure. He met the nun and felt the magnetism of her faith in every nerve of his body. The Lord was surely here! At that moment Umberto Olivieri resolved to give himself to Christ and His Church as a priest. He would investigate every avenue of possibility. Someday, in some way, the ecclesiastical hurdles would be overcome. In later years he would often say, "I am a priest because of Fatima."

From Lisbon his pilgrimage took him to Spain. He visited Zaragoza, Madrid, Avila, Toledo, El Escorial, Burgos, and

Santiago de Compostela. Of the incomparable Prado Museum in
Madrid his diary records the following for August 25: "What
a feast for the eyes and what a relief for the spirit to contem-
plate those majestic paintings! I sat a long time in the hall
dedicated to Andrea del Sarto, where there was a St. Agnes of
which I have long had a photo taken by Mr. W. W. Kent. In
that room I was surprised to find 'La Gioconda.' I did not know
it was at El Prado. It was very interesting to hear that the
'reds' during the revolution had shipped all the most important
paintings to Russia. They were stopped at Geneva. Switzerland
did not allow them any further. They were eventually returned
to Spain. Practically all came back."

Santiago de Compostela, in northwestern Spain, is one of the
great shrines of the Christian world. It honors a tradition that
St. James the Greater, one of the Twelve Apostles, evangelized
Spain in the years following the death and resurrection of Jesus.
Umberto was there on September 5 and made these notes: "I
am just returning from a little stroll through the maze of lanes
and narrow streets of Santiago. I was walking from my inn
toward the cathedral. The city was pretty nigh deserted. A few
people still hanging in the bars and inns, but the streets were
rather empty. Suddenly the main bell of the cathedral struck
eleven with a deep *basso profondo* sound. It did not sound as if
it were striking eleven o'clock but rather the eleventh hour
of an eternity clock. It was not the voice of the present but the
voice of the past, a reminder that centuries have gone and
eternity is awaiting us."

A few days later the traveler was in Lourdes, France. On
Saturday the eleventh he went to Mass at 6:30 A.M. in the
Basilica of the Rosary, remaining there until eight o'clock. "In
coming out I found in the esplanade all the patients in their
stretchers and wheelchairs attending Mass. The weather was
cloudy and it rained intermittently; the stretchers and chairs had
waterproof blankets and hoods which were removed in order
to distribute the Sacred Species. The spectacle was most moving.
It was a pity to see so many creatures, poor wrecks of humanity,
longingly waiting to receive the Body and Blood of Our Lord

and to be consoled by His Divine Presence. Who can deny the reality of the Divine Presence when poor people like these are stretching with heart and soul toward the One who alone can give peace of mind, resignation, strength to bear their infirmities? Now they are absolutely helpless, but they hope for a happiness which will never be marred by misfortune, iniquity or precariousness. Tears were streaming from my eyes and a lump in my throat was choking me and preventing me from repeating the invocation: 'Lord, that I may see! Lord, that I may walk!' "

Also in France, Umberto visited Lisieux (St. Thérèse of the Infant Jesus) and Paray-le-Monial (St. Margaret Mary Alacoque). He found no time to go to his family in Italy, but his brother Dino came to see him in Paris. Umberto returned to Santa Clara by way of London, Dublin and New York.

In 1949 and 1950 he gave some thirty-five lectures, in Italian and English, on the apparitions of Fatima, illustrated by color slides taken on his trip. The lecture tour took him all over California and attracted the attention, notably, of the Oblates of St. Joseph, known among the Italian people as the Giuseppini. Olivieri had been acquainted with some of the priests of that order since his early years in California. In 1950 he was made prefect of his Franciscan Third Order fraternity.

Professor Olivieri was always happy when his relationship with his students could go beyond the mere academic level. Once in a while he was able to share some of his spiritual insights and, hopefully, to bring a boy closer to God. Lester Kerfoot was an example. He became a Catholic after graduating from Santa Clara and entering upon a military career. Umberto was proud to have played a part in his conversion.

The writer of these lines first met Umberto Olivieri late in 1952. My father, an employee of the Bank of America's Santa Clara branch, had known him for many years. I was a student at the University of Santa Clara. At the time I was under instructions to become a Catholic and was attending Mass daily, often in the Mission Church on campus. I could not help noticing the tall, distinguished-looking layman, slightly bent, who moved quietly at the side altars serving the private Masses of the Jesuit priests. I observed that he would usually serve at least two Masses. I knew that he was one of the professors and I was impressed by his piety. Owing to a schedule conflict I was obliged to withdraw after a few weeks from the French class taught by Professor Clemens Van Perre. I was reassigned to Professor Olivieri's class. I remember being a little disappointed that I was forsaking a native speaker of French for an Italian; soon, however, I discovered that Professor Olivieri spoke flawless French. The class met during the first morning period and at times I would be late. I explained that I had wanted to attend Mass and had not arisen in time to go to an earlier Mass. He feigned annoyance, but I could see that he was pleased by my spiritual efforts.

In January 1953 Olivieri passed his sixty-ninth birthday. He had been considering retirement, but in April he signed his contract with the university for the 1953-54 academic year. For some time the Giuseppini had been prevailing upon him to become a public relations man for their order. They planned to build a sanctuary in honor of St. Joseph at Santa Cruz on the California coast. Father Alex Grattarola renewed the invitation.

Umberto Olivieri went to the Trappist Monastery in Huntsville, Utah, to make a retreat. He prayerfully considered Father Grattarola's offer. Yes, that might be a very good thing. Possibly the Giuseppini might even allow him to become associated in some religious way with the order. "All right," he told Father Grattarola, "I'll go with you. But first, I want to spend six months in Mexico."

Seven

BIG BROTHER
TO THE OTOMIS

Professor Olivieri was not too much concerned about his destination in Mexico. He had seen many of the principal tourist attractions on his trip in 1946. This time he would place himself in the hands of the Giuseppini, who were in charge of several missions south of the border, and let them be his guides. He would have the opportunity, surely, to meet Mexican people in their homes and to be refreshed by the spirit of that gracious land so well remembered. Perhaps he would be able to help the Oblate Fathers a little in their work. Then he could return to California and his new career in public relations. And then, who knows?

So it was that Umberto Olivieri accompanied Father Sylvio Masante, O.S.J., on a trip to the Oblate headquarters in Monterrey, Nuevo León, in the summer of 1953. At some point during his short stay the suggestion was made that he might like to work for a while as a catechist in the Valley of the Mezquital in the central part of the country. The Fathers had a mission there for the benefit of the backward Otomi Indians. The old spirit of adventure was never more alive. Of course he would go!

On August 12, from Monterrey, Professor Olivieri sent his letter of resignation to Father Herman J. Hauck, S.J., president of the University of Santa Clara. His words bubbled with the excitement of the new challenge. "Life begins at seventy!" he wrote. The university accepted his resignation without question. Professor Victor Vari was assigned to take his classes.

Umberto soon found himself in Alfajayucan, one of the poorest villages of the Mezquital, where he was to help the pastor, Father Alberto Libardoni, O.S.J. He was given a room in the old monastery built by the Franciscans in the sixteenth century, not long after the conquest of Mexico by the Spaniards. Living conditions were primitive but not at all remarkable when compared to those of the Otomis.

He had never seen such abject poverty in his life. Human beings living in tiny huts made of leaves, eking out a bare existence from the stony soil. An undernourished boy, dressed in rags and a big straw hat, poking a few skinny goats along the dusty road with a sharp stick. A woman of no more than thirty or thirty-five, but with the drawn face and stooped shoulders of advanced age, carrying a load of firewood on her back. A man, slightly less haggard, leading a burro barely visible beneath a huge burden of maguey leaves. Surely this was the land that God forgot! And yet, the people seemed to be happy. No, God had not forgotten them, and it would be his sacred task to help them to know Him better and love Him more dearly.

It did not take Umberto long to adjust to his new surroundings. As he busied himself at the rectory and in the field, he gradually learned more about "El Valle del Mezquital." The name, he found, is given to an area larger than a single valley or even the group of valleys belonging to the basin of the Tula River. It is applied, in fact, to the entire region occupied by the Otomis, including the fringe of mountains on the north and east. The Mezquital lies about one hundred miles north of Mexico City and takes in over a third of the state of Hidalgo, in the west-central portion of the state. It can be divided into two zones, a larger "arid" zone in the north and a smaller "irrigated" zone in the south. In the latter the settlements are somewhat more prosperous and the living conditions a little easier. Umberto was in the arid zone, where irrigation was at that time almost unknown. From a height one could easily count the scant green patches against the dull brown of the natural desert landscape.

The arid zone, with fourteen townships, covers an area of about 3,600 square miles. The population (1960 census) is 177,633, of whom almost half are Otomis. The settlements are small and the dwellings scattered. There are 287 communities in the arid zone without potable water. Ixmiquilpan, with some 15,000 inhabitants, is a "metropolis." Many Mexican *mestizos,* of mixed Spanish and Indian blood, live in the urban area. In Ixmiquilpan Township, however, the population is 96.6 percent Otomi. More than 60 percent of the people of the township are illiterate. Many, especially the women, speak only the monosyllabic Otomi tongue, although an increasing number also know Spanish.

Over 95 percent of the population of the entire Valley of the Mezquital have a monthly family income of less than $120 (1,500 pesos). Well over half of these take in less than $24 per month. Only 14 percent have electricity. Strangely, for all its primitiveness and poverty, the Mezquital as a whole is not isolated. Several major highways cross it, notably the main route between Mexico City and Laredo, Texas.

The Otomi man is head of the family. The woman is virtually his slave. One of her principal duties is to carry water, sometimes from long distances requiring hours of walking. A common sight in the Mezquital is a prematurely aged woman trudging along the roadside carrying two loads: in front, a baby suspended in a sack of burlaplike material; in back, an animal skin filled with water, hanging from a band encircling her head. Once in a while, instead of a skin of water, there will be a second infant on her back, and perhaps a third in her womb. Though the birth rate is high, so is the rate of infant mortality, with an almost total lack of hygiene. Otomis live, for the most part, in natural union, but with a remarkable degree of fidelity of one man to one woman.

The women must prepare meals; care for the home; make, repair and wash the clothing; cut and carry firewood; and take charge of the children, the aged, the sick and the domestic animals. Children are expected to help with the household tasks. Formal education is sporadic, owing to lack of teachers, long distances, inability to understand Spanish, sickness, and sometimes complete absence of incentive.

Often adults and children alike, lacking drinking water or any other liquid, subsist on the fermented juice of the maguey, called *pulque,* quite nourishing but also inebriating. Men can be seen carrying great gourds filled with *pulque* as they wander about the valley. Sometimes a woman will awake in the morning to find her infant lying beside her, dead. The evil spirits are blamed. In fact, the mother herself smothered her baby while rolling about in her drunken sleep.

Maguey is the basis of life for the Otomis. Vast fields of it are cultivated with minimal effort under inhospitable conditions. Rainfall is rare and in most years nonexistent. Maguey leaves provide clothing as well as shelter and nourishment. The fibers are spun into thread which is then woven on primitive, portable looms into a coarse sackcloth called *ayate.* The spinning of thread is such a constant and necessary occupation that even the men deign to take part. Many Otomis carry a spindle and a quantity of fiber with them wherever they go. Weaving is left to the women. (In 1972 the writer purchased an *ayate* about three feet square for six pesos—48 cents—in the squalid village of Xuchitlán, Hidalgo. It had taken four days to make.) Some Otomi women, not the poorest, work also with wool and cotton. They do beautiful embroidery, with flowers, birds, animals and geometrical figures perpetuating the designs of ancient art.

The Otomi men are not idle, although they have plenty of time for *descanso* (rest). They are the social and political leaders of the community. They build houses and corrals, schools and *jagueyes* (water holes), roads and canals. They hunt rabbits and birds. The men organize and direct the frequent *fiestas,* principal means of escape from a monotonous life, at which the women are assigned the lesser roles of cooking and serving the festive meals. Meat, eggs and fruit are enjoyed on such occasions, as well as the usual maize tortillas, beans, chiles and *pulque.*

The Otomis have always been a peaceful, agricultural people, easily conquered by other tribes and herded into a region nobody else wanted. They are of medium stature and bronze color, with finer features than many of the other indigenous races of Mexico. Some of the women are no less than beautiful, in the eye of any beholder. By native heritage they are worshipers of a multiplicity of gods and idols. After the Spanish conquest many became Christians at the hands of Augustinian and Franciscan missionaries. They have preserved their Catholic customs, not unmixed with pagan rituals and superstitions, to the present day, despite centuries of relative neglect by the institutional Church.

These, then, are the people to whom God led Umberto Olivieri. He spent much time in studying them and their pattern of life so as to plan carefully the best ways to gain their confidence. The old linguist began to learn the Otomi language. He already surmised that he would have to spend more than six months there if he were to satisfy himself that he had done any good at all.

In the fall of 1953 my father informed me of my old professor's new situation. I wrote to give him the news that I had entered St. Patrick's Seminary in Menlo Park, California, to study for the diocesan priesthood. He immediately replied from Alfajayucan. This was the real beginning of a firm friendship that was to last for twenty years and that now finds one expression in these pages.

After a month and a half, perhaps, in Alfajayucan, Olivieri made a hurried trip to California to attend to personal and business matters. Upon his return he discovered that Father Alberto had been promoted to the pastorate of Ixmiquilpan. Umberto was not sorry to leave Alfajayucan. In 1953 it was a very primitive place. Humans and animals used the same water hole. The roads were in terrible condition. He bade farewell to the ancient stone church and friary, with its pleasant courtyard dominated by an extraordinary carved stone cross dating from 1560. He said *adiós* to his briefly found Indian friends.

Father Alberto was installed as pastor of Ixmiquilpan, amid much ceremony, on December 12, 1953, the feast of Our Lady of Guadalupe. Bishop Miguel Darío Miranda of the Diocese of

Tulancingo presided. Ixmiquilpan is attractively located on the Río Tula at an elevation of about one mile above sea level. The town is bisected by the Mexico-Laredo highway, so there is generally a bustle of activity. Every Monday is market day. Indians come by the hundreds on foot from villages far and near to buy, sell and trade in the colorful outdoor market. Along the river banks, though, it is peaceful and cool. Hoary trees with massive trunks, silent witnesses of uncounted centuries, relegate to the modern era even the ponderous stone bridge built by the Spanish in 1655. The parish church of Ixmiquilpan, dedicated to St. Michael the Archangel, was erected by the Augustinians in the mid-1500s. Their former monastery, adjoining the church, is a national monument of Mexico, open to the public to inspect its intricate architecture and delicate frescoes. Some rooms are reserved, however, for the use of the parish clergy. Here, with Father Alberto and Father Albino, his assistant, Umberto Olivieri would find a home. (Since the anticlerical revolutions, the Catholic Church has held no property titles in Mexico. The government owns all churches and church buildings and tolerates their use for religious services and activities.)

Umberto's first Christmas in Mexico was something to write home about. This he did, to Mother Agnes of the Santa Clara Carmelites. "We had only three or four days to get settled in the new residence, another old convent, when the Christmas novenas began. I had my share in the doings. My main duty was that of a chauffeur as I had to accompany Father Alberto every night to Tasquillo for the Posada, after the rosary and the Posada in Ixmiquilpan. (Tasquillo is some twelve miles from Ixmiquilpan.) I am sure that you know what the Posada is. It is one of the sweetest things ever devised to impress on the hearts of the faithful the joy of Christians in receiving the great gift of the Redemption. It is a dramatization of the search by St. Joseph for an inn to which to lead his holy spouse, who is about to give birth to the Savior. A most touching devotion!

"My Christmas was a very lovely one. After the closing of the novena in Tasquillo we came back as usual to Ixmiquilpan where we had the 'Misa del Gallo' [Midnight Mass, literally Mass of the Cock] with sermon and reception of the Infant Jesus at the door of the church. Christmas Eve in Mexico is called 'Noche Buena,' the 'good night.' After the service in Ixmiquilpan I drove Father Alberto to a *pueblo* called Lagunilla where another 'Misa del Gallo' was celebrated about three o'clock in the morning. We had a perfectly lovely drive. The night was still and clear. The moon was brilliant and smiled all the way to Lagunilla. Turning on the radio, I tuned in a station in the United States and we heard the traditional Christmas carols, just as if I were at home. I did not feel a bit lonely.

"At Lagunilla we found a large group of Indios waiting for the Mass and warming themselves outside on a huge burning log. The church was crowded, with the poor Indios kneeling on the floor, both old and young people, each one holding in his hand a candle as a mute testimonial of his faith, then forming a line to kiss the Babe in His crib.

"I cannot tell you how lovely are these Masses in the poor churches of the countryside. Every time I assist at one of these Masses I thank the Lord for having given me the opportunity to witness such demonstrations of faith. My place in church is in the presbytery, which is rather elevated from the floor of the church. Most of the time some of the Indios come very close to it and kneel in front of the steps, holding their candles and contemplating the altar and the actions of the priest. The other day there were four women in a line, wrapped up in their *rebozos,* covering their bare feet with their raggedy skirts. Three were rather young and one elderly. My attention was drawn by their composure. They were rapt in contemplation, with an expression between that of a *mater dolorosa* and that of a wise virgin waiting for the arrival of the bridegroom. They were perfectly still, and the candles they were holding gave their faces an uncanny appearance, as if they were really seeing their Beloved. How can one not be impressed by such scenes? How can one not feel inspired by the devotion of these poor, backward, ignorant, and yet understanding and loving people?"

At Ixmiquilpan Umberto sometimes wore the Franciscan

habit, a privilege to which he was entitled as a tertiary member of the order. Casting aside the grand appellations of the past— *Avvocato, Cavaliere, Capitano, Professore*—he asked the people to call him simply Hermano Miguel, Brother Michael. Many undoubtedly thought him to be a Brother of the Oblates of St. Joseph. He was just as often called Brother Umberto or Brother Olivieri.

Early in 1954 Brother Olivieri returned to California with Father Masante for about four months. He delivered a series of lectures on the Mezquital mission, illustrated with color movies and slides he had taken. Donations were asked, and about $1,000 was collected. One of the lectures was given at St. Patrick's Seminary in Menlo Park. The seminarians had little money to give, but Umberto hoped that some might be interested in coming to the Mezquital during summer vacation and working as catechists. The talk was well prepared and interestingly presented. He had some records of lively Mexican dance music to play as a background for the films. He was a little chagrined, I remember, when the seminary rector, a dour man, abruptly switched off the phonograph. The music was "too worldly."

Brother Olivieri made his headquarters for his brief California stay at the provincial house of the Oblates of St. Joseph in Santa Cruz. He informed Father Grattarola that he intended to stay indefinitely in the Mezquital, perhaps for the rest of his life. The Giuseppini would have to look elsewhere for a public relations man to advertise their proposed sanctuary in honor of St. Joseph. The beautiful Mexican proverb had come true for Umberto Olivieri: "Once the dust of Mexico has settled on your heart, you will never be at peace in any other land."

One day he met Father Angelo Verri, a secular priest from northwestern Italy and an accomplished architect. The Oblates had invited him to discuss plans for the sanctuary. In the course of conversation Umberto told Don Verri of his work in the Valley of the Mezquital, of his one-time hope of becoming a priest and the obstacles that arose, of his anguish now because he could not be of fuller service to his beloved Otomis.

"But you *can* be a priest!" said Father Verri emphatically.

"I cannot. I am a divorced man," countered Brother Olivieri. "That does not matter. The Pope will give you a dispensation," replied the architect. "When you get back to Mexico, go straight to the bishop and ask him to accept you for ordination." He went on to tell how Pius XII had granted several dispensations from conjugal bond to qualified professional men in order that they might become priests and ease the severe shortage of clergy in certain parts of the world. He cited the case of a German, born a Jew, who moved to Milan and became the superintendent of that city's electric streetcar system. The man had, at some time in his life, been converted to Protestant Christianity. His son became a Catholic and was ordained a Franciscan priest. The father, moved by his son's decision, became a Catholic himself. He was separated from his wife. With a special papal dispensation, he ultimately entered the Franciscan order and became a priest. "If he could do it, so can you," Father Verri told the excited Olivieri. "You are well qualified."

In the summer of 1954 Father Alberto Libardoni took Brother Olivieri to see Bishop Miranda in Tulancingo. Umberto stated his case. The bishop had heard of him and the good work he was doing. He knew that he was an exemplary Catholic layman. He was sorely hampered by a scarcity of priests in his diocese. Monseñor Miguel Darío Miranda hesitated only a moment. "I'll take you," he said.

All the years of waiting, all the discouraging refusals seemed to fade into insignificance. God had saved Umberto Olivieri for this. His vocation was not simply to be a priest but to be a priest for the Otomis. Priests were plentiful in the United States by comparison with this benighted region. Here he would be inspired to work harder than ever, with the consoling knowledge that his efforts were needed and appreciated.

He addressed his formal petition for ordination to Bishop Miranda on July 20. "From the abyss of my nothingness I venture to present this request, not because I think I am worthy to be raised to the altar to consecrate the Body and Blood of Our Lord and Savior Jesus Christ, but only because I wish to help

innumerable souls to reach eternal salvation, souls who now
have been denied that possibility because of the scarcity of
priests." He enumerated his educational and spiritual qualifica-
tions. He thanked God that he was in excellent health, although
seventy years of age, except for a slight weakness of the eyes.
He submitted humbly to the decision of Pope Pius XII and
confided his petition to the protection of the Blessed Virgin and
St. Pius X. Attached was a glowing recommendation from the
provincial of the Oblates of St. Joseph in Santa Cruz. Official
acceptance by the Diocese of Tulancingo came in November.
The proper documents were forwarded to Rome.

In January 1955 Umberto founded, with Father Alberto's
permission, a praesidium of the Legion of Mary and a fraternity
of the Third Order of St. Francis in Ixmiquilpan.

The work of the young-old lay catechist attracted the attention of W. J. Granberg, a free-lance journalist and a Protestant,
who wrote an article for the American Catholic magazine *The
Reign of the Sacred Heart.* It was published in the June 1956
issue. Granberg named Olivieri "Big Brother to the Otomis."
From the article we learn a typical example of his work:

"Umberto Olivieri, bouncing over a desert road in his station
wagon, lost in a cloud of dust, honks his horn as soon as he
sights the white church at Maguey Blanco. That's warning enough.
Brown legs twinkling in the sun as he runs, a boy who has
been waiting in the skimpy shade of a mesquite tree dashes
to the church and hurries up the worn, stone steps.

"He is Francisco Flecha, eight years old, and he has a great
responsibility. On him depends the success of today, for he must
ring the bell that calls the Otomi children of the desert to
catechism. Francisco, out of breath, grabs the rope that dangles
from the bell and sets himself to swinging like the pendulum
of a clock.

"The bell clangs and the tower seems to tremble. The ringing
notes are so loud they would seem to burst the lad's ears. But
Francisco swings and the bell rings until the dust that hides
Brother Olivieri's car reaches the churchyard. The elderly, gray-
haired man at the wheel waves. Francisco smiles and drops from

the bell rope. It is well. The Big Brother has approved of his ringing. Had he not approved, he would have raised both his hands as a signal for more ringing. But Francisco did especially well today, Wednesday, for this is the day of the surprise gift from Big Brother and not a child must miss catechism.

"Brother Olivieri grasps the small, brown hand in greeting, inspects it closely, and smiles. *'Bueno,* Francisco! Your hands are clean. And your face and shirt also are clean. You are a fine boy, Francisco!' Francisco is made happy by the words of praise, but glad Big Brother hadn't seen him fifteen minutes earlier, at a time when hands, face and shirt gave evidence of an allergy toward water. Other children were not so fortunate. One after the other, as they advanced to greet him, they had to face the keen scrutiny of Big Brother. For most of them he had a smile, but for many there was a scowl that somehow never turned out to be as stern as he tried to make it.

"When the children have passed inspection they gather in three groups, for there are too many of them to be taught effectively by one man. Two young women from Ixmiquilpan, well trained by Brother Olivieri, assist in the instruction. They are bright, intelligent girls and the fact they are interested and eager to help is testimony to Big Brother's missionary efforts in Ixmiquilpan, too.

"The youngsters listen intently. Brother Olivieri puts his message in words and sentences simple enough for the children to grasp easily. For him, religion not only has its mystical side, but its ethical and material. He talks of honesty, virtue and truthfulness, not forgetting cleanliness, tells of Christ and His teachings. Before they know it, the youngsters have learned their catechism, and a lot more.

"After a good solid hour of instruction comes the surprise. Starry-eyed, expectant, the children gather around their friend, eyes on the cloth sack in which he carries such teaching aids as colored drawings of the Holy Family. What will it be today, they wonder—sweets, crucifix, or medal? Slowly Brother Olivieri delves into the sack and the gifts appear. Crucifixes, to wear around their necks instead of a red string! The business of trying to remove superstition from the minds of his little friends is part of Big Brother's job, too.

" 'Remove the red string from your necks,' he said firmly, yet kindly. 'It does no good in protecting you from diseases, no matter what your grandmothers may say. Better that you pray for health than trust in a dirty old string.'

" 'This great thing, too, must come off?' a boy asks, eyes wide. He holds up the dried eye of a mountain deer. It is well known that deer never become ill with a cough, so certainly the eye of a deer will protect a boy from the dreaded disease of the lungs, *verdad?*

" 'Yes, that must come off,' Big Brother says. 'The eyes of a thousand deer have less value than one prayer to Almighty God!' The boy believes and dares to drop to the dust the shriveled eye of a deer.

"The Big Brother plans to stay on in the desert, but if he were to leave tomorrow, the desert and its people would be better for his having tarried there a while. No matter how squalid and submarginal the lives of the Otomis, no matter how near the animal level, Brother Olivieri believes in the oneness of man. He sees in every man a spark of the Divine and nourishes it especially in his particular friends, the children."

Brother Umberto was fond of using movies as visual aids to education, often only a "Mickey Mouse" cartoon to attract a crowd. He equipped his station wagon with portable film and sound equipment for ready use in the field.

With all his time-consuming work he found a few moments each day to keep up his voluminous correspondence. The typewriter was for business letters. Personal messages were carefully written in a clear, steady hand, which only when he was very tired gave slight evidence of his advancing age. To Miss Sigrid Clauson, a sister in the Third Order of St. Francis in San Jose, he wrote on November 2, 1954:

"In this campaigning for Christ we have many enemies to fight. First of all, the not altogether disguised opposition of the government authorities, who, allowing a certain tolerance to the Catholic Church, actually put up all kinds of handicaps and favor the Protestants, whose establishments pass as liberal-cultural missions. There are some sixty Protestants in this zone. Then, the lack of means and personnel at our disposal. Then, the passivity, slothfulness and deceitfulness of the Indians. Last but not least, the scantiness of resources of this country due to the extremely poor communications and the scarcity of water. Add to this the lack of comprehension on the part of our superiors, who are too far away, and you may see that, if it were not for the assurance of protection from Above, there would be plenty of reasons to fold up and quit.

"Just a few days ago there was a procession in honor of the Holy Cross, which moved from a little *pueblo* nearby to go to the top of a lovely, high mountain, known as the Cerro de la Cruz. A High Mass was celebrated there, accompanied and followed by the singing of thousands of people, mostly Indios, who crowded the summit of the *cerro* and overflowed onto its slopes, in a setting of the most superb natural beauty. After Mass a group of Indians, with feathered crests, danced one of their old dances, which lasted uninterruptedly for over an hour, to the monotonous accompaniment of a single violin and the cricketlike sounds of belts, made of pieces of reed, from which were hanging, instead of shells as of old, metal corks from Coca-Cola and other soda bottles. Long live America! The dance was unmistakably aboriginal, but the Spaniards have long since Christianized these Indios, inasmuch as they, the Indios, had on their plumed crests the beloved image of Our Lady of Guadalupe and that of one of their *Cristos,* for whom they have an almost fanatical adoration. Scenes like these, which are quite frequent, are very interesting and make you feel that it is worthwhile to exert yourself for these poor creatures. They are also very encouraging because you feel that the Protestants will have little success in substituting anything else for Our Lady of Guadalupe in the hearts of these simple and primitive, but sentimental, Indios."

Brother Olivieri loved to teach the Indians the hymns in honor of Our Blessed Lady. They seemed to be most prayerful when singing. Many already knew "La Guadalupana," of course.

In addition to his catechetical work, he did the ordinary duties of a lay brother in a religious house—cooking, house-cleaning, etc. He was treated as if he were an official member of the Oblate community. He assisted at Mass from a place in the sanctuary and received Holy Communion daily, to the edification of the entire parish. Perhaps his "apostolate of good example" was the noblest of his works. He enjoyed life in the rectory, although there were the usual conflicts of personalities, found in every religious house, which provided occasions for prayer and penance. The old stone monastery with its thick walls made for comfortable living the year round, cool in summer and warm in winter.

Every six months Olivieri had to leave the country to renew his tourist permit. He decided not to go through the formalities of permanent immigration but simply to return to the United States twice a year, then to reenter Mexico with a new tourist card. Most often he went to southern Texas. On one occasion in 1955 he made contact with the Legion of Mary in Houston. He had written to them for legion supplies. Bernice Walker answered his request. On his next trip north he attended a legion meeting in a small place near Houston called Baytown. There he met George Gamer and Alma McNulty, and later Gene Walden. Members of the legion would help him smuggle clothes for the Indians and other needed articles into Mexico past the border guards. His contact with the Legion of Mary in Houston led to some of the most enduring and valuable friendships of the last two decades of his life, such as his associations with Miss Walker, Mary Peschges, and Genevieve Beck and her mother. Miss Beck's brother Richard, though a man already in his early forties, was inspired to follow his vocation to the priesthood when he saw a man of over seventy making such efforts to become a priest. He is now Father Richard Beck of the Oblates of Mary Immaculate.

The *Patrimonio* is the Mexican governmental agency in charge of the Indians. It is analogous to the Bureau of Indian Affairs here in the United States. Umberto observed that the *Patrimonio* was sending poorly trained nurses into the Mezquital to treat the diseases of the Indians. Often they did more harm than good. Some of them did not understand how to use a hypodermic needle. One Otomi woman almost lost her arm from the resultant infection. Brother Umberto was concerned and upset. He confided his fears to one of the Daughters of Charity of St. Vincent de Paul at the Red Cross hospital in Monterrey. She suggested that he contact the Mother Provincial of the order in Mexico City to see if some hospital sisters could be assigned to work in the Valley of the Mezquital.

On his next trip to the capital Brother Olivieri went to see the Provincial to explain the problem. He did not forget to mention that he had a daughter in the order. Mother was quickly persuaded. Sister Rosa, Sister Mercedes and Sister Margarita were among the first Daughters of Charity to go to the Mezquital in 1955. At first they came only once a month, then every weekend. The Daughters of Charity are the only order in Mexico allowed to wear the religious habit publicly. Nuns ordinarily dress in a variety of lay clothing, priests in black suit and tie. It is said that the exception was made by Dictator Calles, originator of many of Mexico's anticlerical laws, after he was nursed back to health by a devoted Daughter of Charity.

In addition to their work of attending to the health needs of the poor people, the sisters assisted Brother Olivieri with the catechism classes and trained young girls to be catechists. Sister Mercedes remembers that an Otomi girl, little more than eighteen years of age, lay dying on the bare earth floor of her tiny *choza*. It was built so low to the ground that one had to crawl through the single small opening. Brother Umberto asked her if she had yet received "the water" (baptism). She replied that she had, eight days earlier. The pastor was called to bring her Holy Viaticum and Extreme Unction. She died happily that very night.

In November 1955 Umberto made a trip by air to Quintana Roo, an isolated Mexican territory on the Yucatán Peninsula, and to neighboring British Honduras. He was part of a team that brought food, clothing and medical supplies to the area stricken by devastating cyclones. Before leaving he wrote these lines to his friend Gene Walden: "How far the American dollar goes in this country! I had two parties for the Indian kids of Maguey Blanco. I gave to each of eighty kids a *cocol* [an anise-flavored sweet roll] worth five centavos, plus one or two pieces of candy costing six pesos in all. They were perfectly happy. Little Luis, eight years old and very undernourished, was not eating his *cocol*. I asked why. He answered, 'I have it in my pocket to bring it to my brother.' No comment. How beautiful is this unfortunate Mexico! Nobody but God will tear me from it. The more I live here the more I love it."

Wheels grind slowly in Rome. When Brother Umberto returned from the disaster area, he found that the long-sought dispensation had been received. It had taken nearly a year. A priest had been delegated to contact the former Mrs. Olivieri in California to determine that her marital rights would not be infringed. Now remarried, she offered no objection to Umberto's becoming a priest. Other investigations had to be made and character references collected. When all the papers were in order, one of the officials of the Sacred Congregation of the Sacraments had a personal audience with His Holiness Pius XII on October 28, 1955. He recommended that the Holy Father grant the dispensation. The Pope willingly acceded.

Umberto Olivieri should have been elated now that the way was finally open for him to become a priest. Instead, he went into one of those unexplainable depressions that sometimes occur when a person conquers a major hurdle but faces further obstacles. He was afraid that he would not be able to stand the strain of the studies. He was intensely happy doing the work of a lay missionary. He remembered that Pedro de Gante, Mexico's greatest missionary and a cousin of Emperor Charles V, had been a humble Franciscan lay brother. Why should not he, too, be content to remain as he was? He poured out his soul in a long letter to Mother Agnes of the Carmelites of Santa Clara.

Her reply was stern and persuasive: "God has granted you a tremendous grace and the Holy Father a great favor. Do not be discouraged now that it has come and see only the crosses and trials in view. After all, nothing is heavy to pay for the immense blessing and privilege of the priesthood. Your heart should be lifted like a lark, full of fervor and thanksgiving and song. Nothing, no hardships must let you down! Do you not think that God who has been so merciful and so good to you will supply in you and for you all that is needed? Cast out every such thought, I beg you. He will sustain your health. Think back what you have been through in past years. God has given you so fine a mind and heart. Take courage, lots of prayers are with you, dear Mr. Olivieri. God's enemy only does not want you to succeed, and we must defeat him. As you hope to be prepared for a mission life in the priesthood, I am sure the studies would not be too extended or difficult. The simple theology no doubt would suffice. Oh! concentrate on one thought, I beg you. If you get to say only *one Mass,* to offer the Holy Sacrifice once, the whole of life is worth it."

On December 10, 1955, Bishop Miranda of Tulancingo ordered Umberto Olivieri to go to Rome to begin his studies for the priesthood. Within five days he was on his way.

Eight

A PRIEST FOREVER

Umberto Olivieri spent Christmas with the Jesuit missionaries to the Tarahumara Indians in the state of Chihuahua. It would be his last Mexican Christmas for several years. During the first three months of 1956 he presented illustrated lectures in various California cities to raise money for his confreres in the Mezquital. He made his temporary home with Father Savio at Holy Cross rectory in San Jose.

The aging aspirant to the priesthood was left entirely on his own to make arrangements for his studies. He would have to pay his own expenses, buy his own books, find a place of residence. His funds were rather limited, a monthly Social Security check and a small income from some investments. The situation would be complicated by the promotion of Bishop Miranda, his sponsor, to the office of archbishop of Mexico City.

In trepidation, yet filled with confidence in the goodness of Almighty God, Umberto sailed for Italy on April 21. He had not been to his homeland since 1926. First he went to Arezzo to pay a visit to Father Bernardino Banci, O.F.M., who had set him on the road to the priesthood in 1941. The Franciscan monastery was located on the upper floor of a building in the downtown part of the city, above the parish church entrusted to the friars' care. As a tertiary member of the order, Olivieri was invited to stay in the house and eat at the refectory table. One morning he went downstairs for Mass. There, in the church, he observed a bishop confirming a large crowd of children. The bishop moved very slowly. It was obvious that he was extremely old. Upon inquiring Umberto learned that this was Monsignor Emanuele Mignone, bishop of Arezzo, and that he was ninety-two years of age. It was a grace from God. Umberto Olivieri reflected that he himself was only seventy-two and in excellent health. If ordained he could serve as a priest for twenty years and live to be as old as the venerable bishop. The realization gave him new courage.

While at Arezzo he took the opportunity to make a pilgrimage to the mountain of Alverno, the place where St. Francis of Assisi received the holy stigmata, the imprint of the five wounds of Our Lord. "There is a forest of thousands and thousands of gigantic beech trees," Umberto wrote to a Third Order brother, "with some oaks and firs. It is one of the richest forests in all Italy. I spent several hours in that wooded spot. Sitting on the edge of a cliff I admired, speechless, the superb beauty of the countryside, the tiny, silvery course of the Tiber and the Arno, the distant range of blue and purple mountains. Before going into the forest I visited the hallowed places where our father St. Francis prayed, meditated and suffered in union with Our Holy Lord. You have no idea how lonely, cold and inhospitable were those places where the *Poverello* communed with Our Savior. Only his sanctity and his aloofness from the world made it possible. I thought, 'How hard it is to be a saint!' "

Olivieri arrived in Rome on May 6. For two months he made the round of seminaries and colleges seeking acceptance. First he applied to the Seminary of St. John Lateran. The rector told him that it was impossible that a man of seventy-two should share the seminary life of young men in their early twenties. Every contact brought the same refusal. Discouragement began to weigh him down. Sister Josephine wrote to suggest the Beda College, an English seminary in Rome for delayed vocations. He replied indignantly that he would not consider a place "filled with stuffy, old men." In all probability not many of them were much over fifty. He likely would have been the oldest.

While in Rome Umberto had the opportunity to attend the

convention of the Third Order of St. Francis of Italy. He sent a complete report to his brothers and sisters of Sacred Heart Fraternity in San Jose. The gathering closed with a papal audience at St. Peter's Basilica. "The crowd was coming in by the thousands. A murmur was heard, 'The Pope is coming, the Pope is coming.' We all turned toward the entrance of the basilica. On the left side a red curtain was drawn open and Pius XII appeared in his white soutane, carried on his processional throne. He was greeted by no end of vivas, shouts of joy, 'hoch, hoch' of the Germans—almost sailing on a sea of waving handker-chiefs and scarves—while a good many were shedding tears of delight and raising children in their arms to be blessed by the Vicar of Christ. Finally the procession stopped and the Holy Father sat on his throne by the main altar. He delivered a fine address to the tertiaries on the importance of the Third Order as a school of Christian perfection, of real devotion to Mother Church, and of a bold spirit of apostolate for spreading the Kingdom of God. Acknowledging the presence of various groups of foreigners he spoke to them in English, Spanish, German and Portuguese. He seemed to be well enough to carry on the duties of the day. He spoke with energy and warmth, moving his arms to stress the relevant points of his address. After imparting his blessing to all in attendance he passed through the crowd to a real thunder of applause. It was an unforgettable scene. I was really happy to be present at such a function. It has been nearly fifty years since I have witnessed anything like this. I actually met St. Pius X. Now Pius XII, who graciously granted me my dispensation to become a priest, is the fifth Pope I have seen or spoken to in my long life. I may still see another."

When in doubt, make a retreat. One needs peace and quiet to clear the mind and calm the heart. Umberto sought solace in the beautiful mountains bordering the river Anio east of Rome. His wanderings led him to the Franciscan monastery of San Cosimato at Vicovaro, not far from Tìvoli. After a week's retreat he decided that he liked the place so well that he would ask to stay indefinitely. The Father Guardian agreed on a dollar a day for board and lodging. Umberto put on his Franciscan habit and shared the life of the community.

Father Saturnino, one of the friars, heard his story and sympathized with his difficulties. "Let us go to see the bishop," the Franciscan suggested. Monsignor Luigi Faveri, bishop of Tìvoli, listened with an understanding heart. "If it is a question of supervising studies," he said, "I suppose I can do that." On October 4, 1956, Umberto Olivieri was accepted as a candidate for the priesthood in the Diocese of Tìvoli. It was the feast of St. Francis of Assisi.

He was placed under the private tutelage of Father Alberto, one of the Franciscans of Tìvoli. Two or three times a week he would go by bus from Vicovaro to Tìvoli to meet for a few hours with his teacher. Father Alberto gave him many books to read. He observed that Umberto was a highly educated man, well versed in ascetic theology and church history. There was no need to repeat what he already knew. The lessons would concentrate instead on the finer points of dogmatic theology and the practical norms of moral theology necessary for the hearing of confessions as a priest. The studies would encompass a period of a year to a year and a half. In due time and in proper order Olivieri received First Tonsure, the symbolic haircut that marks entrance into the clerical state (he did not have much hair to offer!), and the minor orders of Porter, Lector, Exorcist and Acolyte.

During his stay at Vicovaro, Olivieri expressed an interest in meeting Padre Pio of San Giovanni Rotondo, near Foggia on the east coast of Italy. He had heard much about that famous Capuchin stigmatic who was regarded as a living saint. Padre Pio reputedly had the ability to read the inmost thoughts of perfect strangers. He was known to have withheld the Eucharist from individuals at the communion rail whom he knew to be in the state of mortal sin. One story of Padre Pio concerns a man who drove his wife to the Adriatic coast with the intention of feigning an accident and disposing of his wife in the sea so as to be able to marry his mistress. When they passed in front of the monastery of San Giovanni Rotondo, the wife expressed a desire to go to confession to Padre Pio. She did so and then suggested to her husband that he do the same. Not wanting to arouse suspicion he went into the confessional. Padre Pio startled him by asking, "Aren't you ashamed to come here when in your mind you have decided to kill your wife?" The man was overcome with sorrow. He reformed his life.

Another story is told of a man who was brought by his sister to see Padre Pio. They met the famous mystic, but the man refused to go to confession. The pair left San Giovanni Rotondo and went to visit other churches in the neighborhood of Foggia. At one, a shrine built in a natural cave of pure marble, they encountered a priest dressed in black cassock, ostensibly a secular priest. "Wouldn't you like to see the church?" the priest asked.

"Yes, I would," replied the man, "but I'm not here to go to confession." He wasn't taking any chances.

The priest led him into the sacristy, where there was a large and beautiful crucifix. "Now that we are here in the presence of this crucifix, I am sure that you won't mind answering a few questions," said the priest gently. "Don't you think you ought to be grateful that you were saved from death in the war?"

The man looked mystified.

"Don't you think you ought to thank God that you were cured of cancer?" the priest continued. "Haven't you been somewhat remiss in observing the teachings of the Church? What about your living with that woman to whom you were not married? Don't you think you ought to acknowledge your faults to the Lord?"

The man fell to his knees and begged God's forgiveness.

"In the presence of this crucifix, I absolve you from your sins," intoned Padre Pio, who of course had never left the cloister of San Giovanni Rotondo.

Umberto Olivieri met this penitent sinner and heard the story from his own lips.

Father Mauro, O.F.M., offered to take Umberto to meet Padre Pio. From Vicovaro they traveled through the mountains of the Abruzzi to the Adriatic Sea and thence south to San Giovanni Rotondo. The Capuchin monastery was a place of daily pilgrimage, with people coming from all over the world to see Padre Pio, to receive Holy Communion from his hands, to stand in long lines at his confessional. A group of devotees waited in a monastery corridor. At last the great mystic entered. He greeted each person briefly. Umberto was introduced. "Father," he said, "I am an old man who has come from Mexico to study for the priesthood." Padre Pio raised his hands in holy joy and exclaimed, *"Sia lodato Gesù Cristo!"* ("May Jesus Christ be praised!") When he had finished his greetings and departed, an unmistakable fragrance of roses lingered in the corridor.

Olivieri found time for a brief vacation from his studies. He went to northern Italy. On the way he stopped at Arezzo. At nearby Olmo he met Don Duilio Sgrevi, the parish priest of a small country church, and they became fast friends. Don Duilio took him to the village of Foiano della Chiana to meet Anita Bindi, a saintly Passionist nun who is locally regarded as a mystic privileged to receive revelations from God. She, too, is a stigmatic, although the wounds are not ordinarily visible.

Near Trent, Umberto spent an enjoyable few days with the family of Father Alberto Libardoni, O.S.J. The pastor of Ixmiquilpan was there, too, on one of his rare trips to his native town. Though seventy-three years of age Umberto heard the call of the mountain peaks and did a creditable job of climbing one of the lesser Alps.

Late in 1957 or early in 1958 Umberto Olivieri, having completed his studies to the satisfaction of Father Alberto, O.F.M., and Bishop Faveri, prepared to face a day of oral examinations at the Provincial Seminary of Rome to be eligible for major orders. The old professor was as nervous as many of his Santa Clara students had been as the day of reckoning approached. He had to resort to some stimulant pills to be sure of being mentally alert. The inquisitors were very kind. They knew that his entire priesthood was to be spent among uneducated Indians in Mexico. The questions were easy. He answered most of them

correctly, even astounding his auditors with long quotations
from Holy Scripture and from St. Thomas Aquinas delivered
word-perfect from memory. He passed.

Ordination to the subdiaconate was scheduled. Although the
order has now been suppressed by the Church after the Second
Vatican Council, the subdiaconate was at that time the decisive
step for a secular priest. The subdeacon assumed the obligations
of perpetual celibacy and the daily recitation of the Divine
Office. There was even a "step forward" to be taken as a part
of the ordination ceremony. A retreat was required before taking
the step. Umberto went to a Jesuit house near Castel Gandolfo,
south of Rome. He arrived about five minutes late for the
evening meal. The meal was to be taken in silence, while listening
to readings from pious works. The reader had already begun.
Umberto quietly took a vacant seat near the door. His companions at the table made signs for the elderly man to go to the
head table. The priests at the head table beckoned him to come.
He did not know what to make of this but obediently went
forward and was shown to the place of honor. At the conclusion
of the meal he was asked to say the closing grace. "But I am not
a priest!" he whispered. The dignitaries stared at him in con-
fusion. Someone else said the prayer. As they were marching to
the chapel for the traditional after-supper visit to the Blessed
Sacrament, one of the priests remarked to Umberto, "You are not
a priest? We thought you were the archbishop!"

Father Banci wrote a beautiful letter of congratulation to
Don Umberto on his ordination as a subdeacon. "It all seems
to me to be a dream: our encounter in California, your most
helpful collaboration in my apostolate, our fraternal friendship,
the long and painful and laborious path you have taken to the
priesthood, the hopes nourished, the disillusionments suffered, the
alternate sadness and happiness, happiness and sadness. It is all
a marvelous and mysterious plot by Divine Providence to attract
you, to refine your spirit, and thus to prepare you to enter upon
your ministry." He urged Don Umberto to place himself completely in the hands of his good bishop, not to try to return too
soon to Mexico, to become accustomed to the sacerdotal ministry

in the beneficent milieu of Italy. He invited him to come to the Franciscan seminary near Arezzo after his priestly ordination. "Your presence will be an inducement to the seminarians to persevere in their vocation. It will be more efficacious than a thousand sermons on the beauty of the priesthood."

Don Umberto Olivieri left Vicovaro to make his final preparations for the priesthood at the Benedictine monastery of Santa Scolàstica near Subiaco. There he discovered that Dom Simone Lorenzo Salvi, who had been his luncheon host one day in 1906 on a hiking trip, was now the abbot-bishop of Subiaco. He was old and frail, and a coadjutor abbot-bishop was functioning in his place. Abbot Salvi did not remember the incident, of course, but Don Umberto did, and also that he had almost drowned in the river Anio. Now he was to enter into the priesthood in the same gorgeous valley. Subiaco is an abbacy *nullius,* which means that the abbot of the monastery is also the bishop of the town and a small surrounding area. It is like a miniature diocese. The monastery church serves as a cathedral. Santa Scolàstica houses a school of preparation for young Benedictines and also a seminary for aspirants to the secular priesthood of the abbacy. Here Don Umberto, with the much younger seminarians, would receive training in the Liturgy of the Mass and the manner of celebrating the sacraments.

His stay at Subiaco was sheer pleasure. Often he would awaken in the middle of the night to hear the nightingales calling to one another across the vast chasm of the Anio. He remembered the descriptions of the valley, and of the nightingales, in the lovely books by Antonio Fogazzaro. He recalled his hikes to Bellegra and his hunting trips to La Cervara, happy memories of long ago. Now God had brought him back to become a priest in this ideal spot, favored by the Author of Nature and hallowed by the spirit of St. Benedict.

Don Umberto was ordained to the diaconate on April 20, 1958, in the upper church of the Sacro Speco of Subiaco, the cave in which St. Benedict had lived and prayed. Members of the Olivieri family attended the ordination. A choir of boys sang beautifully. They looked anxiously to see who would be coming up the aisle to be ordained. When they spotted the aged man in his white alb, one boy turned to another and said, loud enough to be overheard by Don Umberto, "Look at that old fellow! I wonder how many times he flunked!" Don Umberto preached his first sermon as a deacon on April 30, the feast of St. Catherine of Siena. He spoke, of course, of the life of that noble woman of God who had influenced his own life so tremendously. The sermon had some of the eloquence of the lecture he had delivered many years before at Dominican College in San Rafael. Don Umberto was happy to be a deacon. He was impressed that St. Francis of Assisi had never advanced to the priesthood, had chosen to remain a humble deacon the rest of his life.

Umberto Olivieri was ordained a priest of Jesus Christ at nine o'clock on the morning of Sunday, June 22, 1958. Bishop Luigi Faveri of Tìvoli officiated. Family and friends gathered in the same upper church of the Sacro Speco. A name was called in Latin: "Humbertus Olivieri." The tall man, vested in alb with the diagonal stole of a deacon, strikingly handsome despite his seventy-four years, answered "Adsum" ("I am present"), advanced to the altar and knelt. After a long exhortation by the bishop, the ordinand prostrated himself on the floor of the sanctuary while the Litany of the Saints was chanted. Then he arose and knelt at the feet of the ordaining prelate. Bishop Faveri imposed both hands on his bald head in silence. All the priests present came forward, one by one, to impose hands. Then the bishop prayed: "We beseech Thee, Almighty Father, invest this Thy servant with the dignity of the priesthood. Do Thou renew in his heart the spirit of holiness, that he may hold the office, next to ours in importance, which he has received from Thee, O Lord, and by the example of his life point out a norm of conduct."

With the words of the prayer resounding in his ears, and his scalp still tingling from the pressure of the ordaining hands, Umberto Olivieri thanked God from the bottom of his happy heart. He knew that he was now a priest forever.

He had reached the top of the mountain.

Nine

TO SPEND AND BE SPENT

Bishop Faveri vested Father Umberto Olivieri in the garments of his new office. The deacon's stole was adjusted to the position in which it is worn by a priest. The chasuble was placed over it. Then the bishop anointed the hands of the newly ordained with oil, proclaiming: "Whatsoever they shall bless shall be blessed, and whatsoever they shall consecrate shall be consecrated." Father Olivieri concelebrated the Mass of Ordination, pronouncing for the first time the tremendous words of Jesus at the Last Supper: "This is My Body. This is the cup of My Blood." Bread and wine are bread and wine no longer, but the Savior of the world offering Himself to His Father on Calvary. "Whose sins thou shalt forgive, they are forgiven them," the bishop reminded the new priest, and the Mass came to an end.

Father Olivieri turned to face his relatives and friends and imparted his first priestly blessing. Then all came forward for the ancient custom of *baciamano,* kissing the anointed hands of the priest. His sister Costanza was there, and his brother Dino. Lello and Carlo and their wives were present. So were the prince and princess of Bisignano—the princess is a sister to Carlo's wife. Many nieces and nephews were there. From the United States there were George Gamer, Gene Walden, my brother Tom and myself. The one person whom Don Umberto most wanted to be present, and who most longed to be, was faraway in Indianapolis, Indiana. The modifications of religious life introduced by the Second Vatican Council were yet to come. For both Sister Josephine and Father Umberto it was a difficult penance, humbly accepted.

The monks of Santa Scolàstica prepared a lovely breakfast. Souvenir holy cards were distributed, some bearing a text from St. Paul: "I will most gladly spend and be spent myself for your souls." (2 Cor. 12:15) One knew that, in choosing the passage, Father had in mind his beloved Otomis to whom he would soon be returning, able to serve them now as never before. One who knew Father Umberto's life story might also have given thought to the words of Our Lord: "Everyone who has given up home, brothers or sisters, father or mother, wife or children or property for My sake will receive many times as much and inherit everlasting life." (Matt. 19:29)

Father celebrated his first low Mass in the abbey church of Santa Scolàstica the next morning. It was a quiet, prayerful gathering, attended mostly by the priests and students of the monastery. A glorious "Te Deum" was sung in thanksgiving at the end.

Tuesday, June 24, was the feast of St. John the Baptist. Father Olivieri chose this day to celebrate his first Solemn Mass in the Church of San Carlo alle Quattro Fontane in Rome, his beloved San Carlino, where as a boy he had often dreamed of being a priest. Don Nazzareno Appodia of the seminary staff at Subiaco was deacon. I was surprised and honored to be asked to serve as subdeacon. Dom Anastasio Lomonte, O.S.B., of Santa Scolàstica was archpriest. All of us wore heavy, highly ornate vestments, redolent of the centuries of tradition that are Rome. Bishop Faveri presided. The congregation included, besides the members of the Olivieri family, several distinguished figures of Roman and Italian society. There was an old school classmate of Father Umberto's who had become a successful canon lawyer and was head of the juridical tribunal at the Vatican. The beloved Professor Raffaele Bastianelli was present. His Excellency Count Giorgio Calvi, husband of Princess Yolanda of Savoy, remarked that Don Umberto gave the final blessing with a wide and energetic gesture, as though he held in his hand the sword of an officer of the army, only now he was of the army of God. Father Riccardo Lombardi, S.J., could not be present, but his brother, who had once been a houseguest of the Olivieris in Berkeley, brought greetings. There were other old friends. Vincenzino D'Arpizio was there from San Benedetto. Dear Matilde Santarelli was one of the first to receive Holy Communion from Father's hands.

Costanza Olivieri Querini gave an elegant reception in her lovely apartment in the Via Firenze. Everyone enjoyed delicious hors d'oeuvres. Bubbling spumante added to the sparkling conversation. It was truly an occasion to rejoice. Costanza delighted in showing visitors an 1888 photograph of herself, Father Umberto, and Dino as children. On the wall of her apartment hung a painting of a priest walking in a desert reading his breviary. It was entitled "The Prayers of One Who Is Far Away." All who saw it thought of Father, soon to be thousands of miles away in the Mezquital of central Mexico, devoting the rest of his life to the welfare and salvation of his Indians.

The newspapers learned that a seventy-four-year-young native of Rome had just been ordained a priest. The wire services picked up the news. Father Olivieri began to receive letters of congratulation from far and near. A lady wrote from Ravenna that she had heard the good tidings on the radio. A Consolata missionary priest reported that he had seen a small item in the weekly paper of Lourenço Marques, Mozambique, where he was then stationed, and had remembered the distinguished professor's visit to Fatima in 1948. Father Angelo Verri, the architect who had played such an important role in Father Umberto's journey to the priesthood, read the news and hastened to send his prayerful good wishes. One of the nicest letters came from a humble widow in Ixmiquilpan, sent on behalf of Father Olivieri's brothers and sisters in the Third Order fraternity he had established there. They looked forward, she said, to his early return to their midst.

Father remained in Italy until late October. He attended the funeral of Pope Pius XII. My brother and I had the happiness of spending a few days with Father in July and August upon our return from a sightseeing trip to other European countries.

He celebrated Mass on August 4 over the tomb of St. Pius X in St. Peter's Basilica. It was my privilege to serve the Mass. Father made a quick jaunt to Lourdes, Lisieux and Paris, then sailed on the *Ryndam* on October 29. Upon arrival in New York he went at once to Indianapolis to see Sister Josephine, a nurse at St. Vincent's Hospital. What a joyous moment it was for both of them when he gave her his first priestly blessing! Then he celebrated Mass. The father from whose hands she had received the chance to live and grow now gave her, from those same hands, the Bread of Eternal Life. He was interviewed and photographed by the Indianapolis newspapers. The Catholic press service syndicated the story and picture throughout the nation.

On to California and a flurry of "first Masses." Father Savio welcomed him back to Holy Cross in San Jose, remarking that he himself, though a few months younger than Father Umberto, had already celebrated the Golden Jubilee of his ordination, while Father Umberto was just beginning his priestly life. There was a Mass at Mission Santa Clara, campus chapel of the Jesuit university, and another at St. Patrick's Seminary in Menlo Park. Beloved Mother Agnes and the Carmelite Nuns of Santa Clara were not forgotten, of course, nor were the Carmelites of Berkeley. A dear, old Protestant friend and former neighbor, Mrs. Anson Blake, attended the Mass in Berkeley. Italian families on the Monterey peninsula were remembered with a visit. Father was reunited with his son-in-law and grandchildren in Truckee. An auto salesman in Reno, Nevada, gave up his commission that Father might buy, for the least amount of money, an eight-cylinder Ford ranch wagon to take him back to Ixmiquilpan and the dusty trails of the Mezquital.

After a short visit with his friends in Houston, Father Olivieri was again among the Otomis in late January 1959. He went to work immediately. On Sunday, February 1, he sang a High Mass in the parish church, at which Father Alberto Libardoni welcomed him officially. "What shall I call this man?" mused the pastor. "Lawyer? Captain? Professor? No, none of these. And," he reminded the joyous Indians, "he is not Brother

Michael anymore. He is now a Father. But he is also a grand-father. He knows the problems of family life. You can come to him with confidence."

Ecclesiastical formalities were quickly settled, and Father Olivieri was released from the service of the Diocese of Tìvoli in Italy to become attached permanently to the Diocese of Tulan-cingo in Mexico. Bishop Miranda's successor in that see, Monseñor Adalberto Almeida, appointed Father Umberto to be chaplain of Nuestra Señora del Carmen (Our Lady of Mount Carmel) on February 20, 1959. This is not a parish church but a public oratory under the jurisdiction of the pastor of Ixmiquilpan. Father Libardoni was glad to grant a certain measure of indepen-dence to Father Olivieri in the pursuance of his apostolate. Father Umberto was to receive no salary. He would support himself and his work by means of his small personal income and donations from American friends.

El Carmen, built in the eighteenth century, stands in a residential *barrio* of Ixmiquilpan within walking distance of the central plaza. The exterior is dominated by two ornate bell towers in front and a handsome dome over the sanctuary. Inside are five elaborate golden altars in Spanish Churrigueresque style. The sacristy walls are decorated with fresco paintings. Here Father Olivieri would be expected to celebrate Mass regularly for the people of the neighborhood, although he would often be called to assist at the parish church. He would also continue his catechetical efforts in the villages of the valley and surround-ing mountains.

Several days each week Father would find it necessary to celebrate two Masses: one at El Carmen or perhaps another chapel in the little city (there are four or five), and one in an outlying settlement. He almost invariably offered three Masses every Sunday and on most great feast days. Mexican custom demands many sung Masses, even on weekdays and as early as seven o'clock in the morning. A typical day might also include a distant emergency sick call, a visit to the hospital or the prison, a round of confessions, a meeting of the Legion of Mary, catechism lessons in one of the villages, with an occasional wedding or baptism or funeral thrown in for good measure. If he were at home, trying to write a few letters or catch some needed rest, he could be sure of several visitors, sometimes a veritable stream of them. His door was always open. Most of the callers were poor people looking for alms or a bit of food or a piece of clothing. They never went away empty-handed. Others came for spiritual advice, which was freely and kindly given.

Father rented rooms in the *barrio* of El Carmen to be close to his people and to share, as much as possible, their way of life. One is reminded of St. Paul's words: "We wanted to share with you not only God's tidings but our very lives, so dear had you become to us." (1 Thess. 2:8) Father lived at several locations, finally settling at No. 21 on cobblestoned Calle Zaragoza. A typical urban Mexican home presents a deceptive appearance from the street. One sees a continuous wall, half a block or more in length, punctuated at irregular intervals by windows and doorways. Upon entering a doorway, one may find himself in a lovely little courtyard with flowering trees and vines. The rooms are arranged around the sides of the patio in such a way that one must go outside to move from room to room. Exterior and interior walls are painted in pastel shades of blue, pink, orange, yellow, green, sometimes purple. Floors are of cement, occasionally covered with colorful tile. Walls, too, are constructed of cement or cement blocks, or of sun-dried adobe brick.

Mary Peschges and Joanne Chambless, of Houston's Legion of Mary, visited Father Olivieri in the spring of 1961. They found him living happily in the spirit of Franciscan poverty, satisfied with the simplest comforts. Bed, table, chairs were purely utilitarian. One "easy chair" was larger than the others, having arms, and was covered with a piece of an old bright blanket and a cushion. His footstool was a wooden box, upholstered in the same fashion. Only his library gave evidence of his erudition. A large bookcase was crammed to capacity with titles in Italian, French, Spanish, Latin and English. These were a mere remnant of the collection he had once owned. On top of the case were piled magazines from all over the world. Other books and papers littered the table in the center of the room. Father was never known for neatness but had the enviable knack of being able to produce with a minimum of searching any item he might need.

"Placidita, Father's seventy-nine-year-old Indian cook, was waiting for us," Mary says. "She still preferred her old ways of cooking. Our meals were prepared in a little thatched lean-to in the corner of the yard on a small charcoal burner. As she finished cooking each dish it was placed on warm coals and covered. The next dish was stacked on top, until all the food was ready. It was a long, slow process to prepare a full meal. There was a temperamental bottle-gas stove in Father's combination dining room-kitchen, but she had no time for it. You had to hit it a couple of times when you turned on a burner before it would light. And then—we got the message, even though she could not speak a word of English—it was much too fast for her. She wasn't about to have the pots boil over.

"Every evening about seven o'clock Father had the rosary in his church. It was attended mostly by the children of the neighborhood. They went through a little ceremony, bringing flowers to Our Lady's altar and singing between the mysteries, much like our May Crowning. He gave them a short talk on Fatima. Prayers were offered for the children of other countries, a different country each evening. It was a simple ceremony, but most impressive.

"On the last afternoon of our visit we observed an unusual amount of activity around Father's place. There was, of course, a line of visitors waiting to see their *Padrecito*. Besides, Silvia, a young Indian girl who helped Father, was holding one of her catechism classes. Then a group of three Indians arrived, a mother, daughter and son. They had walked about twenty-five miles. The son, in his early twenties, had been in a sand cave-in, in which all of his companions were killed. He felt his escape was a blessing from God. He wanted to make his First Communion. Father and Gerardo, the boy who helped him around El Carmen at that time, spent most of the rest of the day with the man, instructing him and reviewing his catechism. Arrangements were made for a place for him to spend the night and a white suit for him to wear the following morning. The two women slept on the floor in one of the vacant rooms near the entrance to Father's patio. The next morning at Mass all three knelt at the foot of the altar, the young man in white shirt and white trousers, the women on either side of him in their Indian garb. It was our last hour in Ixmiquilpan and one we shall not forget."

Father Olivieri enjoyed his status as "priest-at-large." He was happy not to be tied down by administrative duties, except for a few very elementary matters involving his chaplaincy of El Carmen. Back in July 1959 the bishop of Tulancingo had appointed him acting pastor of the parish of Cardonal, to serve for a period of two months during the absence of the pastor. He managed to talk his way out of the assignment, pleading that his brief ecclesiastical education had not prepared him to tackle such matters of administration. In fact, there were several times during Father's priesthood that Cardonal lacked a pastor and was placed temporarily under the jurisdiction of the pastor of Ixmiquilpan. Father Umberto often visited villages in the outlying parts of the Cardonal parish. Cardonal is in the mountains, some twelve miles beyond Ixmiquilpan. It is a former mining area first developed by the Spanish in 1545. Nearby they built the Santuario as a shrine of thanksgiving for their rich discovery. It is still a place of local pilgrimage.

Through the efforts of Father Umberto the Daughters of Charity returned to Ixmiquilpan in 1959. They had not worked there during his absence in Italy. The sisters again attended to the health needs of the poor on their weekend trips. Father induced them to remain for longer periods. He gave them his lodgings and moved to other quarters. The sisters took over an existing private school for the children of Mexican families in the city. In 1960, the third centenary of the death of St. Vincent de Paul, they founded their Ixmiquilpan mission officially. Sister Rosa was named superior.

The same year Father Olivieri began to take an interest in a

Umberto had never seen such abject poverty in his life.

This is the Ixmiquilpan shop of a carpenter who makes little coffins for babies.

A moment after the other picture was taken, an Otomi mother walked by with her baby. She knows that her child may live only long enough to be fitted for one of the little coffins.

Though life expectancy is short, some Otomis do live into old age. This man was so humbly proud of the offering he had brought to church.

Umberto saw in every man a spark of the Divine and nourished it especially in his particular friends, the children.

Maguey is the basis of life for the Otomis. Vast fields of it are cultivated with minimal effort under inhospitable conditions.

At Vicovaro Umberto put on his Franciscan habit and shared the life of the community. *(Courtesy Sister Josephine Tarquini)*

After Father Umberto's first Solemn Mass at San Carlino, June 24, 1958. *Left to right:* Don Nazzareno Appodia, Father Umberto, the author, Bishop Luigi Faveri, Dom Anastasio Lomonte, O.S.B. *(Photo by J. T. Abeloe)*

It was a joyous moment when Father Umberto gave his first priestly blessing to Sister Josephine in Indianapolis.

Father Olivieri celebrated Mass regularly for the people of the neighborhood in his Church of El Carmen.

The children anxiously awaited the end of their catechism lesson, then lined up while Father Olivieri reached into the cookie sack.

The little church of Villagrán built by Father Olivieri. Father and a helper stand in the doorway.

Father Umberto enjoying a moment of relaxation with the Indian girls from the *internado*.

The Indians, whose daily lives are characterized by tremendous hardship, can understand and identify with the sufferings of Christ.

The road to Lagunita was almost impassable, strewn with boulders and crosswashed by deep furrows. A Sister of Charity proceeds with due caution.

Mass was celebrated in an improvised chapel at Cañada Chica. Empty soda-pop bottles made do for candlesticks. *Left to right:* Chucho Trejo, the author, and Father Olivieri in 1971.

Father Olivieri loved to celebrate Mass in the poor,
simple church of Lagunita, which "would have pleased
the first followers of St. Francis."

San Andrés Daboxtha and some of Father's friends

Father Umberto carrying the Blessed Sacrament in solemn procession through the streets of Ixmiquilpan.

A royal visit made the year 1967 a memorable one. In front, with hands on lapels, is Umberto II, former king of Italy. Next to him is Rose Pelleschi. Father Umberto stands in back. The other two men are unidentified.

All Souls' Day is a major feast in Mexico. Father Olivieri celebrated Mass for his beloved people in Villagrán.

The people of Van-
gandhó brought offerings
of candles and fruit on
All Souls' Day.

Father Olivieri with his granddaughter Steffie Anderson and his great-grandson Johnnie, whom he baptized.

Father Olivieri encouraged Enrique Angeles, a young Otomi from Yolotepec, in his vocation to the priesthood. Chucho Trejo stands at right.

The two old-timers, Dr. Goethe Link and Father Umberto Olivieri, enjoyed a beautiful friendship.

Part of the throng that accompanied Father Umberto to his last resting place, March 27, 1973.

The memorial chapel over Father Olivieri's grave is a place of pilgrimage for the Otomi Indians.

neglected *pueblo* about ten miles southeast of Ixmiquilpan on the main highway. The place is called Julián Villagrán. A few squalid houses front the thoroughfare with many more scattered over a wide area among the mesquite bushes and cacti. The community had been without a church since 1930. Father proposed to give the people a place of worship by remodeling the ruins of an abandoned schoolhouse. Construction commenced in June 1961. A year later, on June 19, 1962, the church was dedicated by Monseñor Jesús Sahagún, first bishop of Tula. The Tulancingo diocese had been divided late in 1961, and the Valley of the Mezquital was assigned to the new jurisdiction.

Villagrán and El Carmen were now Father's principal and favorite charges. He would return again and again to the town on the highway. The little church he built, placed like the mother parish in Ixmiquilpan under the patronage of St. Michael the Archangel, was never quite complete to his satisfaction. For one thing, it lacked a good bell for several years. A bell in that desert area is not a luxury. It is an absolute necessity for calling the people together for Mass or catechism. It must be able to be heard over a vast territory. Sometimes, also, fireworks are exploded to attract the attention of the people. Finally, when sufficient funds had been raised, a worthy bell was purchased for Villagrán and a fine tower erected.

Father laughingly described the style of the church as "early conglomeration." It was made of available materials at minimal cost: stone, brick, cement, what have you. Inside is a small statue of St. Michael of gray stone, salvaged from the earlier church. It is very dear to the people, dating back to the days of the Spanish conquest. Father had difficulty in persuading the simple Indians that the statue could not possibly replace the Blessed Sacrament in importance.

In front of the church is a fine esplanade, an inducement to traveling merchants and entertainers to put up their stands and do business. Father Olivieri wrote in a letter to friends: "Some Indians living nearby, who had been under the influence of the Mormons, are now more friendly to the priest, foreseeing the advantages of the vicinity to the church. The World, the Flesh and the Devil are always at work, even in the shadow of the Cross."

Many people gave money toward the provision of a church and furnishings for the people of Villagrán, notably Miss Sigrid Clauson of San Jose; Sister María José Bravo of the same California city; Signora Agnese Querini Passarelli, one of Father's nieces in Italy; Father Lino Gussoni, of whom more will be said later; Mr. and Mrs. John King of Houston, Texas; Mrs. Isabel Dinelli of Sacramento, California; Mrs. Ruth Heintz of Santa Clara, California; the Rosary Club of Monterey, California; and Father Olivieri himself.

Hundreds of cars and trucks each day pass the church on the hilltop beside the highway. People take little notice of it. It is not 400 years old like the great temples of Ixmiquilpan and Actopan. It is not large nor beautiful, though it does have a certain quaint charm. What the passersby do not know is that it stands as a symbol of the love of the "Padre of the Otomis" for his special friends of Villagrán.

Ten

HIS SHADOW
REACHES THIS FAR

The coming of Umberto Olivieri to the Valley of the Mez-quital, and especially his return as a priest in 1959, coincides with the beginning of a spiritual and material uplift in the region. It would be inaccurate to attribute the entire phenomenon to Father Olivieri; there were other factors at work in God's plan. The Oblates of St. Joseph must be recognized for their contribution. The Protestant missionaries, in their own way, have accomplished much. The *Patrimonio* has shown marked improve-ment. New schools have been built and roads bettered. However, Father Umberto did display a love and dedication toward the people of the poorest and most isolated villages that would be hard to equal. By his lectures in the United States, he made others aware of the difficult situation of the Otomis. And he did inspire noble souls to join him in his work in the Mezquital, beginning with the Daughters of Charity.

Father enlisted the aid of young Otomi women through his formation of a Legion of Mary. He was never able to master the intricacies of the Otomi tongue to his own satisfaction. The girls were very helpful to him in dealing with Indian children and adults who could not speak Spanish, and in many other ways. Some of them became real lay apostles. Silvia and her sister Marta were among the first. Eventually they went to Mexico City to be trained as nurses at the Instituto Marillac, a school ad-ministered by the Daughters of Charity. One of Father's favorite helpers was Natalia, who had been one of his first catechism pupils when he too was a lay apostle, bringing with her a little niece named Tomasita, who became very dear to Father.

In 1963 Father sent an Otomi girl named Otilia to Italy to take the course of the Movement for a Better World. He gave up two of his monthly Social Security checks to pay for her passage. Another benefactor took care of her return trip. While there Otilia visited Father's relatives in Rome. She learned the Italian language easily and endeared herself to Costanza Querini and her family. Otilia was thrilled to receive Holy Communion from the hands of Pope Paul VI. She also had the opportunity to see some of the great religious shrines of Europe before coming back to Mexico. A few years later, with Father's help, she founded a small *taller* (workshop) in the poor village of Nequetejé for the manufacture of *guaraches,* the customary footwear of the Indians.

Soon after he returned to the valley as a priest, Father hit upon the idea of taking a few promising girls from the villages to live in Ixmiquilpan where they might learn the Spanish language and the Mexican way of life. Thus, they would be able to raise their standard of living and eventually to secure employment. He gave them the spare rooms adjacent to his lodgings. At times there were three or four Indian girls with him. Sister Rosa observed Father's efforts and was inspired to establish an *internado,* a boarding school for girls, in Ixmiquilpan, to be operated by the Daughters of Charity.

On September 7, 1961, the Valley of the Mezquital came into its own ecclesiastically with the erection of the Diocese of Tula. The cathedral city is located in the more prosperous or "irrigated" zone of the valley. Pope John XXIII appointed a dynamic, young Mexican priest, Jesús Sahagún, to be the first bishop. Full of zeal, Bishop Sahagún immediately put into action his plans for the spiritual and material betterment of the diocese, hampered though he was by lack of funds and scarcity of priests. At the beginning there were only 23 priests to serve a population of 350,000. Father Olivieri and the other priests of the Diocese of Tulancingo working in the Mezquital had been transferred to Bishop Sahagún's jurisdiction.

On her first visit to pay her respects to the new bishop, Sister Rosa told him about her idea of building an *internado* in Ixmiquilpan to train some fifty village girls at a time in modern agricultural methods and the amenities of civilization. The bishop reacted most favorably. He had been thinking of starting a similar project, but now he urged the sisters to go ahead with their plans, except that they were to provide for the needs of the entire diocese, that is, to accommodate no fewer than one hundred girls.

Funds were slow in coming, and construction proceeded on a piecemeal basis. The site finally selected is very near the Church of El Carmen. Father Olivieri recruited the first twenty girls who were enrolled in 1963. They brought others. He asked the sisters to build a small annex with quarters for himself. He would move in at such time as he felt he could no longer live independently. In the beginning the school showed a financial loss but gradually it became self-supporting. By 1967, 145 Indian girls had entered, and 127 had graduated to return to their villages and put into practice what they had learned. The girls are taught reading, writing, religion, Spanish, sewing, cooking, hygiene, land cultivation and animal husbandry. They live in long, narrow dormitories furnished with iron cots. At first they have to be taught to sleep on the beds. They are accustomed at home to huddle on the bare ground in their low, tiny huts. Their first inclination at the school is to sleep on the floor under their beds.

The sisters continued their field work in the villages, especially during vacation periods. Sister Rosa remembers an incident that took place in the settlement of Cerro Blanco, near El Espíritu. "There was a group of some eighteen girls, all about twenty years of age, in whom Father Olivieri was particularly interested. An older man of the village, apparently the mayor, had taught them the catechism from cover to cover in Spanish, although the girls spoke only Otomi. I asked a question from somewhere in the middle of the text, but none of the girls was able to answer it. The mayor suggested that I did not know how to pose the question and that he would do so. The girls were indeed able to answer the questions in sequence from beginning to end, but in fact they had no real comprehension of what they were saying. They had shown a great interest in wanting to learn, for they had committed to memory the test that the man was now giving them. We had a young woman with us who spoke Otomi. She began to explain to the girls all of the doctrine that they had learned and not understood. She used homemade charts that Father Olivieri and we had put together. Immediately we could see the enthusiasm of the group. They laughed and chattered and asked each other questions, as they began to understand for the first time the basic catechism they had learned. Shortly thereafter Father baptized one of the girls (all the others had already been baptized) and gave the entire group First Holy Communion."

One day Father Olivieri had to make an emergency trip to El Espíritu. He described it in a letter to friends: "As I was crossing the market place in Ixmiquilpan, three Indians stopped me to ask if I could go to hear the confession of a dying man. It was exactly 1:15 P.M. and I was thinking of my lunch. But the demand of these people was rather pressing, so I said 'O.K., let's go.' We rode in a pickup for half an hour to El Espíritu. From there we went on a narrow lane through the magueys and mesquites down into a gulch. We drove another half hour to a steep climb which the driver said he could not make. One of the Indians said it was very far and the chauffeur refused even to attempt the climb. We walked. It was pretty stiff and it was a hot day, but fortunately there were some flat stretches now and then, so my legs got some relief. The climb took over an hour. Finally we arrived at the home of the dying fellow. He had fallen from a cliff, and I realized that he had concussion of the brain. With some difficulty, however, he confessed, repented and kissed the crucifix which I placed to his lips. I then administered Extreme Unction. The poor Indian seemed to feel a sense of relief. Upon learning that he was living with a woman but not married, I joined them in Holy Matrimony. The sick man revived and held tightly to the hand of his wife. These poor mountaineers gave me some soup and a few tortillas, which I washed down with half a glass of *pulque,* the preferred drink of the Indians. I hurried down the mountain as I had a class at 5:00 P.M., but did not make it.

"Eight days later, Maximiliano, the brother of the unlucky Diego, came to tell me his brother had died. He wanted me to sing a Requiem Mass at El Espíritu the next day. I acquiesced, feeling very sorry for that family which, in spite of their aloofness from the parish, seemed to be very attached to their Catholic traditions. El Espíritu, even though in a poor zone, has a fine stone bell tower and a very decent altar. The church was nearly full, mostly women and all with lighted candles. There was an atmosphere of tears and pity since Diego was only thirty-five. I praised those poor people for their loyalty to the Church and the love they showed Our Crucified Lord."

In a side chapel to the left of the main altar of the parish church of Ixmiquilpan there is a large crucifix to which the Indians of the Mezquital have a special devotion. It is known as Señor de Jalpan. Originally from Spain, it was brought to Ixmiquilpan in solemn procession from a farm called Jalpan, about thirty miles north of Mexico City, in the year 1770. The crucifix is religiously and artistically executed. The suffering of Christ is clearly etched on the face. Indeed the Indians, whose daily lives are characterized by tremendous hardship, can understand and identify with the suffering Lord.

It is a fact, unfortunately, that many of the Otomis, in their naïvete, worship the crucifix as an idol rather than derive from it an inspiration to adore the Son of God. They claim that the image of Señor de Jalpan has saved Ixmiquilpan and themselves from destruction. Every August there are several elaborate processions in which the crucifix is carried solemnly through the streets of Ixmiquilpan. The people shower it with gifts of flowers and money. One evening procession, accompanied by the explosion of fireworks, lasts from eight o'clock until two the next morning. Every *barrio* of the city is represented, every tiny village of desert or mountains. Local pride begets intense competition.

Father Olivieri had to take part each year in these festivities.

Finally he came to the point that he could no longer tolerate in silence the misguided devotion of the people. He realized that superstitions of long standing are not easily eradicated, but he had to do something. At the same time he recognized that it was not always possible for him and the other priests of Ixmiquilpan to attend the dying in distant locations. The priest might arrive too late. He might not be available when needed, owing to other pressing duties. Señor de Jalpan had to be understood by the Indians as a means to their salvation. Father Umberto remembered that St. Thérèse of the Infant Jesus had once prayed fervently for a convicted murderer in France who was about to be beheaded. She prayed that in some way he would make his peace with God. Minutes before his execution he called for a crucifix, kissed it lovingly, begged pardon for his sins and commended his soul to God. Father Olivieri persuaded the pastor of Ixmiquilpan, Father Benjamín Alcántara (a Mexican secular priest who had replaced the Oblates of St. Joseph in 1962), to preach for several weeks on proper devotion to Señor de Jalpan. The people, he said, must have in their homes a miniature of the beloved crucifix. They must learn to kiss it out of love for Our Lord and to pray, in the Otomi language, *"Pungui Zidada"* ("Lord, have mercy"). In that way, even if the priest were not there, they could attain their salvation through a perfect act of contrition.

Notes for a sermon on the feast of Señor de Jalpan were found among Father Olivieri's effects. From them we can reconstruct most of the homily he preached:

"I have the pleasure and the privilege to present your homage to our most beloved Señor de Jalpan during the annual festivities of this month of August. One question has been on my mind for a long time. I want to know why the people of Ixmiquilpan and all the Mezquital are so attached with such tenderness and devotion to Christ known and venerated as Señor de Jalpan.

"There," he said, pointing to the crucifix, "we have Christ at the highest point of His Passion. What does the Passion of Christ mean for Him and for us? With all the light that the

New Testament does shed for us, the Passion of Christ yet remains a mystery. There is in the story of Calvary something that is beyond our comprehension. And upon this mystery our faith should flourish.

"One aspect of the mystery is the absolute freedom of Jesus before death. As the Son of God He is the Lord of death. But He is bound to it mysteriously because He submits to it freely. He has been sent to conquer death and to give it a new value. 'I am the Resurrection and the Life; he who believes in Me, even if he die, shall live; and whoever lives and believes in Me shall never die.' (John 11:25-26) Every time that Jesus speaks of His death, He illumines it with the light of the Resurrection. 'Destroy this temple, and in three days I will raise it up.' (John 2:19) The predictions of His Passion always end: 'On the third day the Son of Man will rise again.' (Luke 18:33) Nothing is unforeseen in His journey to Calvary. Death comes to Him as the crowning and the conclusion of a life lived solely for this end.

"Christ surrenders Himself to death by the will of the Father. This He accepts as His own will. We submit to death through necessity. He, on the other hand, embraces it with the most profound and intimate love, as we know from the words He uttered before entering the Garden of Gethsemane: 'Greater love than this no one has, that one lay down his life for his friends.' (John 15:13)

"Suffering has no value in itself. What counts is love. If Jesus Christ suffered, it is only because in this imperfect world love cannot be expressed except in terms of suffering. The greatness of the sufferings of Our Lord is the measure of His love. We ought not to think of a God who takes vengeance on One innocent of our offenses but a God who offers Himself completely out of love. The principal accomplishment of the Passion of Christ is love. His death is a requirement of love. The key to a right understanding of this story of anguish is love. 'God so loved the world that He gave His only-begotten Son, that those who believe in Him may not perish but may have life everlasting.' (John 3:16) 'I lay down My life for My sheep.' (John 10:15)

"The nobility of the Passion of Christ consists in this: that it was a faithfulness of love for the Father and for men. By His Blood freely shed for us He merited life, so that each of us can say with the Apostle: 'The Son of God . . . loved me and gave Himself up for me.' (Gal. 2:20) Jesus desired to die, and not only to die but to drink the chalice to the last drop. He wanted to offer a complete and superabundant expiation as a measure of His love. He wished to be not only our Redeemer but also our Model. He desired to explain to us the mystery of suffering. He did not choose suffering because it was something good in itself, but out of love. Suffering without love is no more than fakirism or stoicism. The sacrifice of Jesus is a total gift, because it is total love. If the drama of Calvary culminates in a paroxysm of pain, that is because it is a drama of infinite love.

"Jesus wanted us to see that he who commits a sin is not necessarily the one who atones for it. Christ, the innocent Lamb, took on Himself as a privilege the expiation of the sins of the world. He willed that His friends cooperate with Him in His work of redeeming the world. Thus, in the Garden of Olives, He called His apostles to watch and pray with Him. He laid part of the burden of the cross on Simon of Cyrene. Above all, He wanted His Blessed Mother to unite herself completely with Him in His Passion.

"The sufferings of Jesus and His Most Holy Virgin Mother place us under an obligation of honor to do all that we can to make up for our own sins and those of all our fellowmen. Christians must understand this solidarity which Our Lord established with His creatures. He Himself is the Head of a sinful humanity redeemed. We are the members. Each of us is affected by every sin, whoever may have committed it. And all of us are obliged to offer our sufferings as an atonement for sin in union with Our Suffering Lord."

Padre Olivieri tried to preach in simple Spanish to be understood easily by his hearers, although he never talked in a condescending manner. Occasionally, without meaning to, he probably used terms that were beyond their comprehension. He spent hours in prayer and study in preparation for every sermon,

even though his congregations consisted almost entirely of uneducated and unsophisticated people. He often spoke of suffering,
in that he had learned to accept it in his own life and wanted
the Indians to come to value it as he did. He delivered his
sermons movingly and eloquently, with the frequent hand and
arm gestures characteristic of the Italian people. Once in a while
his fine educational background came to the surface, and he made
literary or other allusions that were totally lost on his audience.
Rose Pelleschi, an American nurse and social worker in
Ixmiquilpan, remembers hearing him on one occasion at El
Carmen preaching to the Indians about Oscar Wilde's *Picture
of Dorian Gray*. Fortunately he told enough of the story to
illustrate the point he was trying to make.

Father spoke with great simplicity, quite oblivious to any
possible adverse consequences of his words. When Marshal Tito
of Yugoslavia received a hero's welcome in Mexico City, Father
was outraged. How could a supposedly Catholic country pay
such honor to a persecutor of the Church! He mounted the
pulpit and blasted Tito. Someone reported him to a local official.
The Mexican government is particularly suspicious of the activities
of foreign priests. Such an incident could have been a cause for
deportation. Thanks be to God, Father Lino Gussoni, a person
of influence in Ixmiquilpan, was able to put an end to the
matter.

Father Olivieri ran afoul of the government on other occasions.
In the village of Cañada Chica he was forbidden to convert a
roofless, concrete-block structure into a permanent chapel because
it was a public building. After some discussion he was allowed
to continue using it for Mass. Once, while visiting Sister Josephine
in Indianapolis, he received an official letter informing him that
he was under arrest for defacing an historical monument. He had
repaired the door of the Church of El Carmen to keep the
goats and dogs from wandering in and out. Sister Jo was aghast.
Father took it in stride. On returning to Mexico he explained
the matter to the authorities and was acquitted on a technicality
that what was fastened to the building by a hinge was not part
of the building.

Father Lino Gussoni, an Italian-born priest of the Archdiocese of New York, came to Mexico in the early 1960s as director of the Mexican counterpart of Catholic Relief Services. Through the years he has done much for the betterment of the Mezquital, including construction of a plant for the pasteurization of milk, canals for irrigation, a large marble factory with machinery imported from Italy, and, most recently, an ultra-modern meat-packing plant for pork products. These are self-help programs, designed to teach the Indians the necessity of work and the value of a peso. Father Lino built a comfortable home on the outskirts of Ixmiquilpan. Here, especially as he grew older, Father Olivieri found a place of refuge from the ordeals of his apostolate. With Father Lino and Rose Pelleschi he could enjoy the stimulating intellectual conversations he craved, an utter impossibility with his Otomi friends. Seldom did he miss a Sunday dinner at Father Lino's. Sometimes the old master chef himself presided in the kitchen as in days gone by. He would often arrive at Father Lino's residence tired, depressed, in poor spirits generally, but he would invariably leave singing cheerfully, ready to take up his work with renewed vigor. A few glasses of good wine, a properly cooked Italian dinner, and the company of devoted friends worked wonders for body and soul.

Father Lino and Rose Pelleschi, like the Daughters of Charity, were inspired to double and redouble their efforts for the people of the Mezquital when they came to know Father Olivieri and to appreciate his example of faith, zeal and self-effacement. Other priests and religious have come to work in the Diocese of Tula, including a number of German-born missionary priests. Some Franciscan Sisters from Denver, Colorado, gave up the comforts of a modern high school in order to open a dispensary and a catechetical center in the remote village of Orizabita, Hidalgo. Perhaps the most interesting religious in the Mezquital are the Little Sisters of Père Charles de Foucauld, who have a tiny cement-block convent in San Nicolás, on the edge of Ixmiquilpan. Their apostolate is one of loving presence. They do not preach, they do not teach. They simply live among the people, humbly sharing their joys and sufferings. They keep a few domestic animals and cultivate a small plot of land. They pedal about the valley on their bicycles, paying cheerful visits to their Indian neighbors. The Otomis can readily see in them a near-perfect example of Christian family life.

Father James H. McCown, a Jesuit priest from Alabama by way of Texas, happened to meet Father Olivieri late in 1961 when Padre Umberto was stationed temporarily at the Tula Cathedral. The old-new priest told Father McCown the story of his long road to the priesthood. The Jesuit Father was inspired to return to the Mezquital sometime later to work as a missionary for a brief period. He tried to interest two divorced Catholic men of his acquaintance in studying for the priesthood, with the hope that they, like Father Umberto, could receive the necessary dispensation to be ordained. At first they showed considerable enthusiasm, but unfortunately they did not persevere.

Bishop Sahagún asked Father Olivieri to contact some of the bishops and priests of the American Southwest for donations toward the building of a seminary in Tula. Father took the assignment very seriously. One bishop offered him $100, but Father would not leave his office until he had raised the ante to $300. Another bishop could give only $100 but promised to pay for the entire seminary if he won a court battle with the heirs of a wealthy Texan who had willed part of her fortune to the diocese. Monsignor John D. Connolly of St. Vincent de Paul parish in Houston was particularly generous and helpful.

It was about this time that the Catholic bishops of the world assembled in Rome for the Second Vatican Council. Bishop Sahagún honored Costanza Querini by calling at her home. He assured her that Father Umberto was in good health and enjoying his work.

Father Olivieri traveled to Houston at least twice a year for the renewal of his tourist permit. Because of the difficulties sometimes experienced by priests in Mexico, he never declared himself to be a priest but rather a professor. His clothes were inconspicuous with the exception of a French beret worn at a surprisingly jaunty angle. Father always made contact with the Legion of Mary on these trips. In 1962 the legionaries helped him to establish a Mission Club to gather prayers and financial support for his activities in the Mezquital. Members were asked to send a dollar a month to help pay the small salaries of the lay catechists. The first bank deposit was made on June 15 in the amount of $89. Father offered Mass regularly for his benefactors. At less regular intervals, although several times each year, he wrote a letter which was duplicated and mailed to the members of the club. Mrs. Bonnia Knipp headed this effort at first. Ultimately the club was led by Miss Genevieve Beck, who continued it until Father's death. Sometimes Father Umberto would remain in Houston for a longer period of time, especially if his services were needed there, or he felt the necessity of a little vacation. In March 1963 he gave a week-long mission for Mexican-Americans in Houston. He often spoke at the seminaries, with the result that several seminarians spent their summer holidays helping him in the Mezquital, along with an occasional priest.

Whenever possible Father would travel from Houston to Indianapolis before returning to his work. These visits with Sister Jo were his principal tie with the past, although he did keep up a regular correspondence with other members of his family. He made many friends at St. Vincent's Hospital. Usually he would arrive unannounced in a taxi from the Indianapolis airport. This might be at any time of day or night. If he came in at six o'clock in the morning, he would go to the chapel, kneel on the floor behind the back pew which Sister always occupied, and surprise her with a hearty "Hi, Jo!" If he arrived in the middle of the night, he would go to the emergency room, where the nurse on duty would find him a spare bed in which to spend the night.

On one occasion he showed up about 11:30 P.M. The regular nurse was not on duty. The night supervisor gave him a private room on the second floor but failed to explain the situation to the nursing staff. An alert aide noticed that the room was occupied and presumed that the gentleman was a new patient. She brought in a chart, a blood-pressure gauge, a thermometer, etc., and went about her regular routine. "No, you cannot wear those pajamas, you have to put on a hospital gown," she admonished the elderly "patient." "I'm not a patient, I'm Sister Jo's father!" replied Father Olivieri. It seems that many disoriented patients were assigned to that floor. The nurse's aide was sure this was another. She insisted on the hospital regulation, and Father thought it better to submit peacefully. He got into the hospital gown and went to bed. A few minutes later the aide returned and popped a thermometer into Father's mouth. He took it out, protesting, "Don't take my temperature! I'm not a patient, I'm Sister Jo's father!" She tried to calm him and reassure him that everything would be all right. At this point he decided that he might as well pretend to be sick. He began to describe all his symptoms. She listened patiently, recorded his blood pressure and temperature, brought him ice water, showed him the light switch and the call button, and promised to look in on him all through the night. Finally, the night supervisor came in to see that he was comfortable. The two enjoyed a hearty laugh. The supervisor then explained the situation to the aide and commended her for being so vigilant. On subsequent visits Father would always take time to look up that aide and tell her, "I'm feeling much better because you took such good care of me that night."

On another visit he abruptly sprang from his chair under the impetus of a sudden inspiration. How many times had he been to Indianapolis, and he had never seen the famous automobile racetrack. "Jo, I must go there!" was the signal that some way must be found to gratify his wish. A few strings were pulled, and before long Father Olivieri was riding at breakneck speed in one of the racing cars. Another day, while visiting friends on a nearby lake, he took the wheel of a speedboat and opened the throttle all the way, meanwhile singing at the top of his voice the gayest Italian arias he could remember. Father could generally be relied on to do the unexpected. After delivering a lecture to an Indianapolis audience, he was entertaining the group with some lively Mexican songs. Noticing a young Mexican lady in the auditorium he called her to the stage, and together they danced a Mexican dance to the accompaniment of his singing and snapping of fingers.

In 1963 Father took a special interest in an Indian girl, María Luisa Ramírez, about fifteen years of age, from his favorite village of Villagrán. She was paralyzed from the waist down, having been shot through the spine by a brutal man when she resisted his advances. Father arranged for her to be transferred from the small Ixmiquilpan hospital, where she was not receiving proper therapy, to Mexico City. In letters to the Mission Club he reported her progress:

"In dismissing her from the Ixmiquilpan hospital I found that the poor child had no proper clothes, only an old, torn kimono. So before going into Mexico City we stopped in Ciudad Satélite at one of those supermarket places and got her a new kimono. Then we bought a bottle of Eau de Cologne and a case with soap and comb, all for five dollars. All of these things were badly needed, and she accepted them with pleasure and gratitude.

"María Luisa is now in the Escandón Sanatorium of the Daughters of Charity and is attended with love and efficiency by sisters, doctors and nurses. Through some very kind friends we obtained a secondhand wheelchair, and the poor girl now roams around the hospital, in the corridors, garden and chapel, interested and observing everything. She smiles with a smile that tells that she has not lost faith in life. This poor, little Indian who did not know anything about faith and supernatural life, who hardly ever heard the name of God mentioned, is now learning to pray, and she prays because she sees that the Blessed Virgin and Our Lord Jesus Christ, whom we taught her to love, are not forgetting her. The other day one of the hospital staff urged her to come out of the chapel after a sufficiently long visit. But María Luisa would not budge. She kept repeating, *'Otro ratito! Otro ratito!'* ('Let me stay a little longer!') Finally, but reluctantly, she left.

"While thinking of this poor girl and the many changes that have come recently in her life I came across these words from the spiritual writings of Father Grandmaison, S.J.: 'Zeal for the things of God gives you the joy of sowing seed in deep, rich soil, of watching the little green stalks of wheat spring up eagerly, then swell, ripen and become golden.' Dear friends, pray that our little green Indian stalk may ripen and become golden for the glory of God."

It was early in January 1964 that Father Olivieri, approaching his eightieth birthday, agreed to go with the Daughters of Charity and some lay catechists, Indian girls, for a month-long mission at La Lagunita, an extremely isolated place way up in the mountains north of Ixmiquilpan. The road was almost impassable, strewn with boulders and crosswashed by deep furrows. The sisters and their helpers set out in a jeep to get everything ready for the mission. Father was to follow a day later on horseback.

A hired car brought Father to the foot of the grade, where Saturnino, his Indian assistant, was waiting with the horses. Father had scarcely mounted when his horse shied, throwing him against some large rocks and bruising his ribs severely. At first he thought they were broken. The agony was so great as to preclude the possibility of continuing on horseback. Father tried to rest while Saturnino went to get Respicia, an Indian girl who was one of Father's favorite helpers. Then, with Father in the middle supported on one side by Saturnino and on the other by Respicia, they began to walk to Lagunita. Along the road they were surprised to encounter Sister Rosa in the jeep. She had been stalled overnight by a flat tire and a torrential rain. Father had a bumpy, painful ride the rest of the way to Lagunita, but it was an improvement over walking.

Lodgings had been prepared for Father in an abandoned schoolhouse. The weather was miserably cold and windy, and the only available blankets were very light. The accommodations for the sisters and the lay catechists were even more primitive. Father suffered terribly from the pain of his bruised ribs but bore it bravely in the spirit of penance. Another part of the schoolhouse was used for cooking. It was impossible to keep the smoke from drifting into Father's improvised bedroom, with the result that he had to keep the window open in spite of the cold weather. "If the pains of Purgatory are anything like this, God help us," he thought. A day or two later a pickup arrived from Ixmiquilpan, driven by a friend who had learned of Father's predicament. He urged Father to return to the city. It would have meant the end of the mission, for there was no other priest to hear the confessions, celebrate the Masses, give the First Communions, perform the baptisms and rectify the marriages. Father Olivieri remained in Lagunita.

The sisters planned a special celebration for Father's eightieth milestone on January 12. On the morning of the great day the entire mission team arose before dawn to serenade him outside his bedroom window with the lovely *mañanitas,* a touching Mexican custom on birthdays and important feasts. Then a kid goat was slaughtered and barbecued in an earth pit filled with hot stones and covered by maguey leaves. Natalia and Sister Dolores prepared a kettle of rice and another containing a thick meat soup or stew. They covered the receptacles and left them to simmer over the fire in the semioutdoor kitchen while they went to Mass in the village chapel. Imagine their dismay when they returned to find that wandering goats had overturned one of the kettles and gobbled up every bit of the rice, while a pack of dogs had gone into the stew pot and enjoyed a real feast in Father's honor! The sisters were inconsolable. Father just laughed. He remembered the time that he was bending over a sick, old woman to anoint her. Just then a goat entered the hut and butted him so hard from the rear that he went sprawling almost on top of the woman. Now, to add insult to injury, the barbecue was raw. They ate what they could of it with plenty of hot sauce and managed to put together a sort of pie from cookies and cheese. The festive meal may have been a disaster, but the joyousness of the occasion saved the day. It was concluded, naturally, with the happy singing of Italian and Mexican songs.

On the thirteenth Father was able to write a few cheerful lines: "My health has had a remarkable improvement through rest and a heavy woolen blanket which Saturnino bought for me in Ixmiquilpan. More acceptable than anything else is a glorious sunshine which dispelled all the gloom, shivering and uncertainty of the past week. This place is perfectly beautiful when the sun shines, all surrounded by peaks and mountains covered with pines and other fine trees. On the north side it opens toward a deep and long valley which at this time is submerged in a sea of fog, while higher up we are enjoying perfect weather. At night the valley looks like an extensive lake enclosed in a crown of mountain peaks.

"After my birthday dinner I said another Mass in the evening.

The Indians filled their little church both in the morning and in the evening. I cannot describe adequately my emotions and intimate joy when I celebrate the Holy Sacrifice in a place like this, so faraway from the voice of the civilized world, in a very poor, simple church, where the Lord seems to come more willingly to give consolation to these poor semisavages who, in spite of their ignorance and superstitions, are hungry for the light of Truth.

"On these last two mornings, having established the Blessed Sacrament upon the altar, I have participated in the morning prayers of the sisters. What a strange and mystic feeling you get when you pray in the cold, silent morning in a church that would have pleased the first followers of St. Francis. There is just the sanctuary lamp and two or three *veladoras* to enlighten the darkness of this dismal place, with holes on the ceiling and in the walls letting in the cold, shivering morning air."

The sisters and their helpers spent much of their time rounding up children for First Holy Communion. When he felt better, Father accompanied them to La Pechuga, a village even beyond Lagunita. The journey had to be made on foot. There they found Juanita, a teen-aged Otomi afflicted since the age of two with osteomyelitis. They persuaded her mother to allow her to be taken to the hospital in Ixmiquilpan. Eventually she joined María Luisa at the Escandón Hospital in Mexico City where she received expert treatment.

Father Olivieri had been to Pechuga at least twice before, once in the company of Father Alberto Libardoni and three others. Father Alberto remembers that Father Umberto had forgotten his *sombrero* and that his nose became as red as a cherry. Nonetheless, he was in great spirits, riding on the back of a donkey, singing all the way down the mountainside, his voice echoing in the valley below. Father Olivieri wrote to an Italian friend, shortly after another trip to Pechuga, made alone: "I was exhausted, but happy to have spent a night with those poor Indians who said, 'Remain with us, *Padrecito.*' Perhaps I will return there on Christmas Eve for the *Noche Buena* to take a little comfort to those poor souls. Jesus will be with us and

Mary Most Holy will help us to feel the happiness of Christmas in our hearts. How much beautiful poetry there is in the world when one loves Jesus."

In writing to friends about his difficult ministry Father often added "Don't think that I am a martyr!" or some such line, lest his readers imagine that he was complaining about his lot. To the Mission Club he once wrote that his work was becoming "a physical effort which, even when borne in a spirit of charity, leaves me in a state of semiprostration from which I recuperate but slowly. All this sounds very tragic, but I am enjoying my life in spite of it all, age included, and then not all days are the same. When the sun shines you forget the cloudy days and look for some shade. So we go on with hope and confidence in Divine Providence."

Father Miguel Baca, O.F.M., wrote of Padre Olivieri in his column "Life Is for Living" in the June 1965 issue of the *St. Anthony Messenger,* a Catholic magazine published in Cincinnati, Ohio:

"His zeal and perseverance are what should awe, inspire and even shame me, and, in truth, they do. But what I really marvel at is his quiet, gentle humor. He's able, even, to laugh at himself. Someone sewed a huge, round, black patch on the seat of some worn gray trousers of his. Seeing him from behind, I was struck with the thought that he looked like a motorcycle rider, and I told him so. He laughed, felt the seat of his pants, laughed some more and agreed he likely did. Another time he brought me provisions to an outpost and, in a voice loud enough for what natives were around to hear, said: '. . . and I brought you some *baptismal water.* Thought you might be running out of water for baptisms!' With a huge wink he handed over a corked Pepsi-Cola bottle full of bourbon.

"The sun is setting here in Laredo, Texas, as I write this, and I know full well the sun sets to the west. The Mezquital is to the south and many miles away. Yet, Padre Olivieri's shadow reaches this far. Across the mountains, plains and deserts it reaches this far."

Eleven

HE FOUND GOD
AND HIMSELF

Not long after the mission at La Lagunita and the celebration of his eightieth birthday, Father Umberto Olivieri spent forty days in southern Texas giving lectures on the Mezquital and collecting alms for the construction of the seminary in Tula. He had the privilege of making a Cursillo in Galveston. This is an intensive experience of Christian community lasting three or four days. It is of modern origin, from Spain. The beauty and joy of living in Christ is demonstrated and actuated through singing and dancing and relaxing with one's brothers in Christ. There are talks on the basic truths of our faith, yet the overall tone of the encounter is congenial and lighthearted. Holy Mass is celebrated each day, as are the Way of the Cross and the recitation of the rosary. A priest serves as chaplain of the Cursillo, but the management of it is entirely in the hands of laymen, since it is for laymen that it is principally intended. The theme song, "De Colores," traditionally sung in Spanish even at English-speaking Cursillos, tells of the beauties of God's creation and, by implication, of the overwhelming beauty of a life lived in and with and for Christ. Father Olivieri went away from his Cursillo refreshed and renewed.

Upon his return to Ixmiquilpan he took part in a ceremony for the dedication of some ten new, very simple houses built for the Indians at a place called La Estancia, up in the hills near Tlacotlapilco. For centuries they had been living in primitive maguey huts. Father Lino Gussoni was responsible for the improvement. He and Monseñor Jesús Sahagún, bishop of Tula, combined the inaugural with a First Communion Mass for forty children who had been prepared by two American Papal Volunteers. Father Olivieri shared the experience with Mission Club members in one of his letters:

"The Mass was celebrated in the open in front of an old ruined chapel under a bower of branches, with a large attendance of parents and friends of the children. It was a dialogue Mass with frequent hymns and invocations. The bishop spoke very humbly and paternally to the children and all the audience, creating an atmosphere of otherworldliness enhanced by the bareness of the surroundings and the poverty of the majority of the people. When Communion was being distributed we were all thunderstruck to see a very old Indian woman dressed in white going to receive. She was eighty-one years of age, feeble and slow in her motions, but her face was bright and smiling after the Mass. It was her First Holy Communion!"

There were forty or more such population centers in the 900-square-mile parish of Ixmiquilpan, providing more than enough work for the pastor, the assistant pastor (at the times when the parish had one), and the aged chaplain of El Carmen. Yet Father Olivieri's priestly heart reached out still farther. One neglected *pueblo* that caught his attention was San Andrés Daboxtha, in the parish of Cardonal, accessible from Cardonal by a road thick with dust or, if it had rained, thicker with mud, or directly from Ixmiquilpan by an even worse road, steep and littered with sharp rocks. An ancient stone church half in ruins, a primary school, and the usual wide scattering of maguey-leaf *chozas*—this is San Andrés Daboxtha. The pastor of Cardonal visited only once a year, and not always then. He celebrated the festive Mass on St. Andrew's Day, received the humble offerings of the Indians, and returned to his parish headquarters.

During a time in 1964 when Cardonal was temporarily without a pastor, Father Olivieri was called to San Andrés. He had not been there long before he discovered that there were dozens of babies unbaptized, more dozens of older children and even adults without First Holy Communion, many couples living together without the blessing of the Church. Here was a place that needed a mission, and soon. He would return.

"Sister Rosa and the other sisters were available," Father wrote to the Mission Club, "for it was the last week of their September vacation. On Wednesday a big party of nuns and cooperators entered San Andrés as the vanguard of the Army of Christ. I was not able to be there until Thursday evening. We illustrated the purpose of our presence, and immediately Sister Rosa and her aides set themselves to getting the data for the proper canonical procedure for the baptisms. You have no idea what a crowd of people came to San Andrés! Some of the people came from La Florida, another little *barrio* about three hours' walking distance up in a nearby valley. Between Saturday and Sunday I baptized eighty-four little pagans! Babies and even children around ten years of age. It is almost unbelievable to relate that after our departure, following months and months of drought, a very abundant rain fell on the arid extension from El Sauz to Pozuelos and farther on. Again last week another beneficial rain fell upon that scorched land. The Indians were happy and felt that the Lord loved them for having hurried to the church in order to have their children baptized."

Father returned many times to San Andrés Daboxtha. He fell totally in love with these poorest of the poor, and they with him. He always brought material gifts as well as spiritual blessings. Sometimes it was powdered milk for the children, sometimes sacks of beans, or seeds to be planted, or clothing to replace their dirty rags. He kept one or more women in Ixmiquilpan constantly busy sewing for him.

When possible, he celebrated Christmas Midnight Mass at San Andrés. Way up in the mountains, with only candlelight for illumination, it was easy to imagine the first *Noche Buena* in Bethlehem. "One of the most inspiring Masses I ever celebrated in my priestly life," he wrote. "The little, dark church was filled to capacity with the poor, rough Indians, all aglow with the expectation of the descent of the Holy Babe from Heaven.

They did not know too much about the Gospel's description of the birth of Christ, but they were, in all their simplicity, ready to adore their God become Child."

María del Carmen Ledesma was working as a teacher's aide in Ixmiquilpan in 1965. Father Olivieri had first met her in 1954 when she was a small child and he a lay catechist. He prepared her for her First Holy Communion. Now, eleven years later, he persuaded her to leave her position and to enter the community of the Daughters of Charity. Sister María del Carmen is one of four girls from the Mezquital whose vocations to the religious life were encouraged by Father Olivieri.

In August 1965 Father was traveling by bus to Monterrey, accompanying two Mexican girls from Ixmiquilpan who were going to work for a while in Texas. Someone would meet them in Monterrey, but their father would not give them permission to go unless Father Olivieri escorted them that far. At a place called Ciudad Mante the old priest stepped out of the bus for a few minutes. Alas, he slipped on a wet cement ramp and fell, breaking four ribs and skinning his left hand badly on the gravel. The bus was ready to depart. The girls washed Father's hand with some water that was available. It was contaminated. By the time the bus reached Monterrey an infection had set in and traveled up his arm. He went immediately to the Red Cross hospital of the Daughters of Charity. They called Dr. Martín Martínez, a specialist in traumatology, who, after several days of intensive treatment, was able to save Father from the much-feared amputation of his arm. Nonetheless, he had to spend a month in the hospital. A few days after his arrival he experienced the same feeling of darkness that had overcome him during the tonsillectomy in San Francisco forty years before. When the hospital chaplain came to bring him Holy Communion, he requested also to be given the Holy Anointing of the Sick. With the reception of this sacrament for the first time, Father Olivieri became a member of that exclusive group in the Western Church who have received all seven sacraments.

Christmas 1965 saw Father Umberto celebrating three *Misas*

del Gallo: first at San Andrés Daboxtha, then at the *internado* in Ixmiquilpan, and finally "at the *pueblo* of Villagrán where I arrived after 4:00 A.M. Expectancy was indescribable with explosions of love expressed in the usual Christmas songs and others in the Otomi language. I did not go to rest until 11:00 A.M. after a complete blank night. I paid for it with two days of helplessness. Then again, I found myself obliged to celebrate Midnight Mass on New Year's at the *pueblo* of Remedios, followed by three Masses in the parish and another three Masses on the feast of the Holy Name of Jesus. Next Monday, I was on the intransitable road to Lagunita up in the Sierra for two Masses for the Indians in that lovely but lonely spot. The little church of Lagunita, at last, after unending efforts, has been completely restored through the help of some friends, especially by some seminarians of St. Mary's Seminary in Houston. Not much rest was available with the confessions and Masses for the Epiphany and the First Friday of January. I reached my eighty-second birthday on the twelfth, but now I am afraid I shall have to renounce much of my activity. My heart, I am sorry to say, does not seem to stand any more the pleasant and inspiring work of the mission. The doctor says I must give up my tourist excursions to the mountains and sit down, thinking more of my sins and being ready for 'future events.' "

The above lines were written from his bed at the Hospital Escandón in the Tacubaya district of Mexico City. He found himself there as the result of his first heart attack, suffered early in January 1966. Word reached Sister Jo in Indianapolis. She secured permission from her superior to visit Father, her first trip to Mexico. With Sister Helen, her English companion, she arrived at Hospital Escandón in March. Father had improved greatly and was shortly to be dismissed. He "had someone buy a beautiful bunch of red roses," Sister Jo wrote. "When we entered his room, he slowly rose and with some of his former gallantry presented them to us. He stood weakly but erect and oh, so happy!"

The sisters went home with him to Ixmiquilpan and were deeply moved to witness the loving welcome he received from his people. They strove to touch him. Some kissed the ground on which he had walked. They who had little enough for themselves brought him simple gifts: an egg, a fruit, some tortillas. The sisters were taken for a tour of his missions. Sister Jo was anxious for his welfare should he be taken ill again. She returned to Indianapolis totally reassured. He had the promise of any number of homes if and when he should have to give up his humble lodgings: with the Daughters of Charity at the *internado*, or at Hospital Escandón, or at the Instituto Marillac, or at the provincial house of the order; with Father Lino or Rose Pelleschi; at the seminary of Tula where, in the words of Bishop Sahagún, "his presence would serve as an inspiration for the young men."

Father Olivieri did begin to exercise a little restraint in his relentless activity after the stern warnings of his failing health and the even sterner warnings of his doctors, but never would he give up his missionary work as long as the Lord provided him strength. He would continue to live the maxim of St. Ignatius of Loyola: "We must fight and not heed the wounds, toil and not seek for rest." He still drove his own car, even buying a new one when it became necessary. Eventually he would allow himself to be chauffeured by others. He began to take most of his meals at the *internado*. After a few years he moved into the quarters there that had been built especially for him.

We do not propose Father Olivieri as a candidate for instant canonization, although we could observe that if he is not in Heaven there is little hope for the rest of us. He had his human faults, and he was the first to admit them. His unflagging zeal led him to become extremely demanding of others. In his defense, though, it should be stated that he never asked anything of another that he was not willing to do himself. His outspoken criticism of those who sought an easier way of life probably cost him several friendships. Also, especially as he grew older, he was perhaps somewhat overly sensitive to the apparent ingratitude and lack of appreciation displayed by many who were the beneficiaries of his sacrifices.

The Christmas spirit of 1966 overcame Father's better judgment, as usual, and he celebrated three Masses, one after another, in three different places during the night. He did obey the doctor by not going to San Andrés Daboxtha, much as he wanted to. "I was up until five o'clock in the morning. I slept only one hour, and the rest of the day was spent receiving friends, mostly kids, who came to present their wishes and gently hint that they expected some toys, which they got."

Bishop Sahagún, taking into account Father's age and health, had by this time excused him from the obligation of attending the dying outside the city of Ixmiquilpan. Father did not always make use of this concession. "After all," he said, "how can I be at peace with myself when a dying person is lying there waiting for divine help? How strange is the life of these Indians. Even though they lead what you might call an uncivilized life and away from the Church, when death threatens them they send, if it is at all possible, for the priest, even though he may be many hours and many kilometers away. In their own way they believe in Jesus Christ. On the point of death, being invited by the priest, they recite a few words of repentance, fondly kiss the crucifix, and close their eyes in the hope of opening them in a more pleasant world. Great is the mercy of God!"

The March 1967 issue of the magazine *Esquila Misional*, published in Mexico City, contains an article entitled "Los Apóstoles del Mezquital" in which there is a summary of Father Olivieri's interesting life and an account of his charity toward the dying in the remote back country. The article goes on to point out that Father was not alone in his loving ministry, that each of the priests, sisters and lay apostles of the Mezquital had his or her own story of bravery and dedication.

It was in the same year that Sister Josephine, while recovering from a serious illness, was directed by her superior to begin work on a biographical sketch of her foster father. Others, including friends in Houston, had in the past urged him to write his memoirs. He had reacted with indifference. To Sister Jo he now showed kind, but firm, opposition. "Writing about my life is ridiculous!" he replied to her request for information. "Who am I to deserve such notice? My early life was not

guiltless. If now I am not living the usual humdrum existence
of the average, mediocre Catholic, my life is still very far from
what it should be for a real Christian loving his Divine Savior
sincerely and perseveringly. My life is not like what we read in
the lives of the Saints. Please reread St. Paul's First Epistle to the
Corinthians and meditate on his words. 'I have planted, Apollos
watered, *but God has given the growth.*' (1 Cor. 3:6) Writing
about me is certainly an exaggeration. At least wait until I die as
a martyr! Remember the Italian saying: *'La vita al fin è il di loda
la sera.'* ('The life of a man is to be praised only after he dies,
just as the day is to be praised only after the sun has set.') If you
must write, limit yourself more or less to an obituary, for my
sun will soon be setting."

Sister Jo, however, persevered in her task and produced a
delightful reminiscence of fifty-seven manuscript pages, on which
this book is, in part, based.

Father often told his friends that though he would not court
martyrdom, he would die a happy man if God chose him to
be a martyr in the Mezquital. In a sense he did die a martyr's
death, for he gave the last iota of his strength for his least
brethren. But that is getting ahead of the story. He was still
very much alive in the eventful year of 1967.

"I must tell you," he wrote excitedly to Sister Jo, "that last
Thursday, March 2, we had a very extraordinary person visit us.
No one less than the ex-king of Italy, Umberto II! He was
returning from a long safari through Guatemala, Honduras,
Yucatán, Mexico City and other places. Dino, unfortunately,
was not with him.

"When he was in Mexico City he got in touch with the
bishop of Tula through the Apostolic Delegate and announced
that he was going to Tula and expected to see me. I was
ready to go to Tula and present myself to pay my respects
when the king notified the bishop that he wanted to come to
Ixmiquilpan. Just think! So, with Father Lino and Rosa Pelleschi,
we made our strategic plan.

"Rosa and I got into the kitchen and, under my direction
and intervention, we prepared a regular Italian dinner or 'classy

lunch' with a Risotto alla Piemontese (my masterpiece, leaving aside my modesty), then a veal roast (Rosa's achievement), with several vegetables, all this preceded by an antipasto Italiano. During the meal an exquisite Bordeaux wine, Chateauneuf-du-Pape (1962), was served. The dinner attracted the attention and the repeated approval of His Majesty and the guests. Then we had a Gâteau St. Honoré, coffee, and finally, champagne. All this, first class, because of Father Lino. Some of his powerful friends in Mexico were both generous and helpful.

"After dinner I had to make a speech, which I delivered with several references to my early years when Umberto I, his grandfather, was king. They say that I spoke well. I was in good spirits, probably due to the excellent wine. Later we were submitted to a regular machine-gunning of photography. Almost everyone in the party had cameras and wanted the historic event in color and in black-and-white.

"I must not overlook the fact that Rosa prepared a beautiful table with flowers, nice linen and, because we had nothing better, 'silver' of stainless steel. The room was lovely with a real Spring sunshine and red flowers so beautiful that the king was actually pleased and kept admiring it for some time.

"Afterward we went to Orizabita to meet the American sisters and to see the new dispensary which is in the process of being built. On the way back the king stopped to greet the good Sisters of Père de Foucauld, with whom he spoke for quite a while in his impeccable French.

"The king was very pleased. On departing he embraced me. He had kissed me when he arrived. He is most pleasant. Yesterday he sent a telegram of thanks and best wishes. Father Lino and Rosa were exceedingly pleased. You can imagine!"

The royal visit ended, it was back to work for Father Umberto. In June he wrote a touching letter to Sister Gerald LaVoy, O.P.: "I happened to be actor and witness at a wedding ceremony which filled me with real exultation. A young Indian couple in a forlorn place called Estancia were going to celebrate their wedding. The chapel where the ceremony was to take place was extremely poor, nothing but an old barn where there was only a rudimentary altar and a few miserable paintings. The floor of this chapel was of pure dirt and so unkempt that I advised the bride to lay some newspapers on the place where she was going to kneel in order not to soil her wedding garment.

"All around poverty was conspicuous; not the least sign of mundanity was in evidence. The bride, cute in her simplicity even though not too poor, was escorted by some girl friends dressed up after a fashion and cheered by some acquaintances who had come from Mexico City where the girl had been working for some months. I was so impressed with the shepherdlike simplicity of that ceremony, by the innocence of that couple and the atmosphere of sincerity prevailing there, that I was inspired to make a lively sermon on the sacrament of marriage, the like of which I had never spoken before. Later some of the witnesses praised me for the unusual lucidity of my Castilian.

"I generally do not like to celebrate marriages. I feel always a great pain in my heart for the happiness dreamed of by the spouses and the inevitable deceptions and sorrows of the married life, but that day I was really happy to be a priest and prayed with fervor for the happiness of that unsophisticated and gentle Indian couple. May the good Lord protect them until the last day!"

Nineteen sixty-eight was also to be a momentous year for Father Olivieri, for it held in store two unexpected and very enjoyable trips. Early in January he received a surprise visit from Father Elwood LaVoy of Las Vegas, Nevada, whom he had known since the younger priest was a small child. There was a grand tour of Mexico City and of Ixmiquilpan and its environs, and then Father LaVoy invited his old friend to return with him to Las Vegas. There Father Umberto celebrated his eighty-fourth birthday. He preached one Sunday at all the Masses in Father LaVoy's parish, St. Francis de Sales, and two weeks later at St. Joan of Arc parish where his friend Monsignor Thomas F. Collins was pastor. He had known Monsignor Collins as pastor of Little Flower parish in Reno. The prelate introduced the missionary of the Mezquital at all five Sunday Masses as "unique in the Catholic world." More than $1,000 was donated by enthusiastic parishioners of the two churches for Father to take back to his Otomis. Between the two preaching assignments he made a quick trip to Reno and to California to be reunited with his family and old friends. His grandson John Firpo had already achieved local fame as a television personality in Reno.

Then, in July and August, Father traveled to Europe to take part in the pilgrimage to Fatima organized by the Blue Army of Our Lady. He attended a seminar for priests and laymen on the message of Fatima. Afterward he proceeded to Rome for a reunion with his family. He offered Mass again at San Carlino and at the Sacro Speco of Subiaco. He was present at a public audience with Pope Paul VI at Castel Gandolfo. With his brother Dino he journeyed to Arezzo to visit Don Duilio Sgrevi and other friends. At the house of Anita Bindi, the mystic of Foiano della Chiana, Father was surprised to meet Eva Tamburini, sister of the man who had painted his portrait in 1909. He had not seen her for many years. She gave him a book on the life of an Italian Augustinian priest, a late vocation like himself, named Father Augustine of Christ the King.

On August 16, shortly before his return to America, Father Olivieri celebrated Mass in the Sacred Heart chapel of the Basilica of Santa Marìa Maggiore. He remembered that he had once given his mother a picture of the Sacred Heart of Jesus bearing the words: "Your heart is enough for me." Now he offered the Mass for the happy repose of her soul, within sight of the home where she had lived and he had been born. He was overjoyed to imagine that she, in spirit, might be looking out of those windows across the *piazza* to see her priest-son celebrating Mass for her.

The writer of these pages first visited the Mezquital in November 1968. I was fortunate enough to arrive on the Day of the Dead, All Souls' Day, which is a major feast in Mexico. My reception committee consisted of a delightful eleven-year-old boy, Jesús Trejo, called Chucho, and several of his friends. Chucho was now Father's principal helper around El Carmen. We left almost immediately for Villagrán, where Father and I concelebrated the traditional Mass in black vestments. My first sight of the devoted Otomis, in their stark poverty and utter simplicity, is one I shall remember for life. We returned to Ixmiquilpan before setting out for our second Mass at Vangandhó. Upon arrival in the city we were shocked to learn of the sudden death of Señor Eulalio Trejo, Chucho's father. He was over eighty years of age. We went on to Vangandhó, leaving Chucho at home to comfort his mother.

That evening many people assembled in the Trejo home to recite the rosary for the deceased. The house was only a few doors from Father Olivieri's rented rooms on Calle Zaragoza. The body was laid out in a simple casket in the main room, surrounded by candles. We knelt on the hard cement floor. As the rosary continued into litany after litany, my knees began to buckle. I wished that I could sit down, as some of the older women were doing. Then I looked at my eighty-four-year-old brother priest, almost half a century my senior, kneeling straight upright without support. I felt ashamed and continued on my knees.

My time, unfortunately, was severely limited, and I had to leave Ixmiquilpan the next day. After celebrating Mass in El Carmen I drove Father to the parish church so that he could show me the ancient temple and former monastery. There we said good-bye. He declined a ride to his quarters. As I drove away I saw him vault the low wall surrounding the church and, with long strides, walk energetically back toward Calle Zaragoza.

Father's semiannual visit to Houston in May 1969 coincided happily with the ordination of Father Joseph F. Perez, Jr., in Guardian Angels Church, Pasadena, Texas. Father Joe had been one of the seminarians to spend his summer holidays assisting Father Olivieri in the Mezquital. Father Umberto enjoyed the bilingual ordination ceremony very much, even the modern music rendered by a mariachi band with trumpets and guitars.

Soon after his arrival in Houston Father grew homesick for the Valley of the Mezquital. He was inspired to write these words: "When you are accustomed to walk, ride on horseback or in a car in an immense desert territory like the Mezquital, even if you are alone, you feel you are in the presence of God. You can admire the beauty, the majesty, the grandeur of the mountains with their peaks projecting into the incomparable blue of the Mexican sky. Then, when all of a sudden you find yourself in the center of a monster city like Houston, where everything is the work of man—that man, mechanical, artificial, mysteriously powerful and anonymous, running precipitously and disappearing in unattainable distances—you feel hopelessly lost, and you ask yourself, 'Where do these people put their God?' Inevitably you feel lonely; you want to return to your desert and to your mountains. So do I. Houston—grand, busy, expanding with gigantic babelic building increasing the wealth of your million inhabitants—I admire you! Yet I would not change you for my mountains where I can say I find God and a little bit of myself."

Father was happy at the arrival of two Mexican priests, Missionaries of Guadalupe, who stationed themselves at San Nicolás. These younger men were better able to stand the rigors of the mountain villages. Now he did not have to feel guilty that he could no longer visit the remote spots as frequently as in the past. He would concentrate instead on places closer to Ixmiquilpan—beloved Villagrán, of course, and the neighboring *pueblos* of Cañada Chica, Xuchitlán and Pueblo Nuevo, the last "an unfortunate, primitive place where on Easter Sunday 1968 an old grudge about some land abusively occupied by some of the wealthier inhabitants burst out in open armed conflict. Ten peasants were killed. The government sent troops for the maintenance of order. Now the calm is reestablished, but fire is still under the ashes. The people were happy for the Mass. They sang nicely during the service. I promised to spend a whole week with them in order to teach them how to say the rosary for the souls of their departed."

He also visited Nequetejé, in the other direction. There he learned that one of the workers in the sandal factory "who lives in a kind of hut hardly fit for animals has a wife and four or five children. The food in this hut is barely sufficient for a meal each day for each person—one or two tortillas with a *mopal* leaf, rarely with beans, and a glass of *pulque* when available. And yet this family, upon the death of a woman neighbor, gave shelter and food to the lonely infant she left behind. Amid so much misery, heroic charity can still be found among these Indians."

It was late in 1969 that Father Umberto received notification of the death of his older sister Costanza. He was comforted that he had been able to visit her just the year before.

Father had a clever way of using any available pretext to help his people overcome the spiritual inertia so characteristic of them. For example, the following handwritten receipt, found among his papers, is dated May 8, 1970, and is signed by a man who apparently was Father's driver: "Received of Padre Humberto Olivieri the sum of three hundred pesos [$24] as a friendly loan to help buy a tire for my old pickup. I, for my part, promise to assist punctually and faithfully every Sunday morning at Holy Mass, with my little children and my wife Cándida, and to accompany the padre on Sunday to Villagrán or other nearby places without charge."

In September 1970 Father Olivieri came to California to take the place of a vacationing priest, Father George Marenco, an old friend, at his little country parish of Linden, near Stockton. Father Umberto was there for about a month. Sister Josephine came out from Indianapolis to keep house for him during part of this time. "I was able to cook for him, wash his dishes," she writes. "In fact, I was just his little girl once more. I treasure that memory more than you can fathom." He traveled by bus to Truckee, where on October 11 he baptized his own great-grandson John Joseph Anderson, the son of Steffie Firpo Anderson and her husband, Duane.

Father extended his trip into a brief vacation, most of which he spent with me at St. Perpetua's rectory in Lafayette, California. We visited many of his old friends, especially in the San Jose-Santa Clara area. I took him to see his daughter Jessie's grave at St. Mary's Cemetery in Oakland. He had not been there since before he was ordained a priest. Tears flowed down his cheeks as he raised his hand in blessing over the little plot. During the long hours of driving here and there, we talked of his life.

At length I was able to convince him that writing his auto-biography would be a service to the Church, that it might plant the seeds of a priestly or religious vocation in the hearts of other "senior citizens." I promised him my assistance and sent him back to Mexico with a cassette recorder for the dictation of his memoirs.

Sister Jo and I both visited him early in 1971. On this occasion I was introduced to a new field of his endeavor, the village of Yolotepec, along the main highway not far beyond Villagrán but in the parish of Lagunilla. There I met Enrique Angeles, a young Otomi with aspirations toward the priesthood. Father encouraged the boy's vocation because of his piety and zeal and his fluency in the Otomi language. He looked upon Enrique as his potential successor. Enrique was doing an admirable job as a catechist in his home town of Yolotepec. On my return to California I found a Lafayette family willing to sponsor his seminary education. He entered the seminary later that year and, at this writing, continues to advance toward his cherished goal.

As time went on, Father grew more and more dubious about the autobiography, as his letters to me revealed. The recorder broke down and could not be repaired. He read the lives of other late vocations: the book that Eva Tamburini had given him; *No Shadow of Turning,* the life of Kent Stone who became a Passionist priest; *I, a Sinner* by Father José Mojica of the Franciscans; *A Rebel from Riches* by Father Bede Reynolds, a Benedictine monk. These stories impressed him greatly but only served to convince him that his own life, by comparison, was not worth writing. It looked as though the project would have to be abandoned. Through it all Father retained his sense of humor, as he wrote: "You in your goodness and friendliness want me to cover speedily the road to notoriety, even if I prefer to make myself a den between the roots of one of those big *savina* trees along the Tula River."

For several years Father had gone frequently to the Bene-dictine monastery near Cuernavaca for a few days' retreat. He found the atmosphere peaceful and congenial. There, in 1971, he met a Xaverian Sister, a Japanese born in Mexico. He found her to be intelligent and deeply spiritual, and they struck up a friendship immediately. She told him many things about Japan and the depressing conditions there, with a large percentage of suicides, insanity, etc. The youth, he learned, were without faith, any faith, and given to drinking and use of drugs. "She has very generous ideas and would like to go to Japan, following the ideal of St. Francis Xavier," he wrote. "I am quite enthused by her ideal and, old as I am, I would like to give my little bit of love for the Japanese. Dying in Japan as my last act of love for the pagans would be a Xaverian closing of my life that would justify the story of my life, which as it stands now would be a saltless account in the midst of millions of stories of martyrs and missionaries. Crazy idea as it is, it is an idea worthy of St. Francis Xavier, S.J. God will tell." I commended him for his undying spirit of adventure but gently reminded him that the Otomis were depending on him. He had to agree.

In January 1972, shortly after the celebration of his eighty-eighth birthday, Father Umberto received word of the death of his youngest brother Màssimo in Brazil on December 30. He had not seen him for over fifty years. Màssimo was only seventy-three. He had named one of his sons Humberto.

Father Olivieri was always interested in new movements in the Church, although he never departed from his basically conservative approach to Catholicism. In June 1972, while visiting Sister Jo in Indianapolis, he attended a gathering of 10,000 Catholic Pentecostals at Notre Dame University. He was impressed. For several years, on each trip to Indianapolis, he had called on Dr. Goethe Link, a distinguished retired surgeon and a Protestant, four years older than himself. The two old-timers enjoyed a beautiful friendship. They shared many interests, especially a love of nature. They would sit for hours admiring the birds and the flowers on Dr. Link's Indiana farm.

Father now allowed himself much more leisure time at his home in the *internado,* although he was still likely to be interrupted at any moment by an Indian caller. Chucho Trejo slept every night on a cot in Father's quarters, in case Father should need him. Father enjoyed sitting on the porch, feeding and watching the tropical birds. "This old field hunter and lover of nature," he wrote, "feels pangs of remorse for having killed so many of those plumed beauties—woodcocks, quail, grouse, ducks, snipe, doves, blackbirds, etc.—those precious animals that St. Francis called 'Sister Birds.' Now the 'old man' is gone and the 'new man' is appreciating those creatures under another facet, which is a realization of the eternal beauty of the immense and beneficent Creator."

On September 29 the celebration of the annual patronal feast of St. Michael the Archangel at Villagrán was carried out with unusual solemnity. Father was assisted by Father Lino and Father Francisco Hagemeier, a German Divine Word priest who was the new pastor of Lagunilla. An Otomi girl translated into the language of the people Father Francisco's inspiring Spanish sermon. In November the writer paid Father Olivieri a week's visit, at the end of which he returned to California with me. It was to be his farewell trip to the United States.

We spent a busy but very enjoyable month together at St. John the Baptist parish in El Cerrito. Sister Jo joined us for two weeks. Every available moment, whether we were driving to visit family and friends or just relaxing in the rectory in the evening, was spent tape-recording Father's recollections of his long and fascinating life. At times it was painful for him to remember. He would remind me that one of the consolations of Purgatory, according to Dante, is obliviousness of the past "by drinking the waters of Lethe." We made a total of over sixteen hours of recordings. It was unthinkable that he should spend Christmas away from his beloved Otomis, and so he flew back to Mexico in mid-December.

He returned to the coldest winter he had ever experienced in the Mezquital. The half-clothed Indians suffered terribly, many falling victim to influenza. His Christmas Midnight Mass at Villagrán was not as well attended as usual, probably due to the cold. He celebrated a second Mass on Christmas Day for the prisoners in Ixmiquilpan. On January 12, 1973, he quietly observed his eighty-ninth birthday. Every Sunday he continued to go to Villagrán for Mass, and also on Thursdays for catechism, assisted by Sister María Guadalupe from the *internado*. He began construction of an addition to the Villagrán church, "a room where we can gather the girls who want to learn to make their own clothes. We will place there one or two sewing machines and engage a sewing teacher to help the girls."

Father Olivieri's last letter to me, dated February 27, 1973, was one of the last letters he ever wrote. It concludes almost triumphantly: "I'll say good-bye now because I am expecting to go to Cardonal to see Padre Patricio García, who is ten years younger but not as tough as your loving *hermano* Umberto."

Twelve

TO DIE IS GAIN

"Remember, man, that thou art dust and unto dust thou shalt return." With these stern words the priest, each year on the first day of Lent, reminds the faithful that life is short. Then he traces a cross of blessed ashes on their foreheads.

Father Umberto Olivieri marveled that the Lord kept him alive and in reasonably good health, able to continue his apostolate beyond the normal span of years allotted to man. Perhaps it was because he had made such a late start. He realized, of course, that every day was "borrowed time," and he often thought of his death. At times the prospect seemed to frighten him. At other times he faced the inevitable "last call" with serenity and resignation, waiting patiently and peacefully for Sister Death, as the followers of St. Francis term it so beautifully. The words of St. Paul held special meaning for the aged "Padre of the Otomis":

"I have full confidence that now as always Christ will be exalted through me, whether I live or die. For, to me, 'life' means Christ; hence dying is so much gain. If, on the other hand, I am to go on living in the flesh, that means productive toil for me—and I do not know which to prefer. I am strongly attracted by both: I long to be freed from this life and to be with Christ, for that is the far better thing; yet it is more urgent that I remain alive for your sakes." (Phil. 1:20-24)

March 6, 1973, was the day before Ash Wednesday. Father Olivieri took his principal meal at midday with the girls of the *internado*. He had bought a cake as a gift for them. That afternoon he went out to do some of his apostolic work, perhaps to visit with some poor or sick person. He returned, perspiring profusely, and unthinkingly he removed his shirt. Before long he began to have great difficulty in breathing. The sisters put him to bed and called a doctor. Despite an injection to relieve the congestion he spent a miserable night. He was unable the next morning to go to the parish church to help with the services. His own physician, Dr. Villalobos, who was always astounded at his vitality, came to see him and gave him another injection. By evening he was still no better. The sisters arranged for an ambulance to take him that night to Hospital Escandón in Mexico City.

Notwithstanding the best of care his condition worsened on Thursday. The staff doctors did not expect him to live through the night. The hospital chaplain, a Salesian priest, gave him the Holy Anointing of the Sick. Sister Josephine was telephoned in Indianapolis. When she and Sister Helen arrived on Friday afternoon, quite expecting that he had already gone to Heaven, they were heartened to find that he was a little better. By Monday he was much improved. This writer flew to Mexico City on Tuesday. I greeted Father on Wednesday morning and found him in excellent spirits, if a little pale. He embraced me vigorously, making a typical observation, "Guess I almost kicked the bucket!" I spent a week visiting him. We even talked a bit about his biography, on which I was ready to begin work. He loved to be taken in a wheelchair to sit in the hospital courtyard, wrapped in a blanket, with his old *sombrero* on his head. The sun warmed him; the flowers and birds enchanted him. One day he was cheered by a bedside visit from His Eminence Miguel Darío Cardinal Miranda, archbishop of Mexico City. As bishop of Tulancingo he had given Father his chance to become a priest. Father's strength seemed to be returning. We had been warned that death could come at any time, for his heart was weak and a blood clot had formed in his lung, but I still held out a tiny hope for his recovery. I felt it necessary to return to California on Wednesday, March 21. Sister Helen also flew home to her work in El Paso, Texas. Sister Jo remained with Father.

On Sunday night Father's regular night nurse was not on duty. Another woman was taking her place. Father slept only at intervals. They spent much of the night in conversation. The nurse had been away from the Church for many years. Before morning Father had heard her confession and restored her to the life of grace. When the chaplain came to bring him Holy Communion, she joined him in receiving Our Eucharistic Lord.

Father was radiantly happy on the morning of Monday, March 26, 1973. He beamed as he told Sister Jo of what God had accomplished through his sickbed ministry: "I am a priest always, up to the last." He enjoyed a hearty breakfast, then dispatched his daughter to the nearby Mercado de Tacubaya to buy a pair of comfortable leather *guaraches.* She located the desired footwear but was short of Mexican money and went back to the hospital to get some. On entering Father's room she found Sister Teresa, several nurses, two doctors, and the Salesian priest with him. "Father had definitely changed. He waved to me smiling. I rushed to embrace him. His smile became ever more serene. He closed his eyes and, as I whispered into his ear, 'Father, go in peace,' he gave a sigh . . . and he went to God." It was 10:20 A.M. and the beginning of eternity.

His last trip back to his beloved Otomis was made in the company of his daughter and her sisters in Christ of the order of St. Vincent de Paul. They arrived at El Carmen at 6:30 P.M. His simple, wooden coffin was lifted high with a note of triumph, placed before the altar and opened. The customary priestly vestments were not to be seen, not even a stole. Father's body was clothed instead in the rough Franciscan habit he loved, as he had requested. In death he was just Brother Michael again.

Hundreds of Otomis thronged the garden of El Carmen and the nearby streets. Now they crowded into the church to file past their *padrecito,* sobbing and placing flowers in his casket. An honor guard of men took positions. All night the church was filled. The rosary was recited over and over again. I arrived at two o'clock in the morning to find Chucho Trejo manning the bell rope. The bells were tolled at intervals, to be answered by the bells of the other churches and chapels of the town. The bell was rung at Villagrán, too, ten miles away. Some claimed that they could hear it all the way to Ixmiquilpan. Embalming is unknown in rural Mexico. The funeral was scheduled for eight o'clock Tuesday morning at the parish church. El Carmen would have been entirely too small.

At 7:30 A.M. the casket was carried up Calle Zaragoza, past the house where Father had once lived. All along the route the doors were hung with black crape. The bells tolled. The procession moved slowly and silently. Everyone walked behind the casket, including Sister Jo, supported by her metal crutch. At the parish church Bishop Sahagún of Tula, a visiting bishop from Zacatecas, and Father Lino took their places at the altar, along with over two dozen other concelebrating priests. Señora Berta Fregonese was there from Mexico City. The distinguished Mexican lady, widow of an Italian, was Father's special friend and his hostess whenever he was in the capital city. Her grieving chauffeur Mario was at her side. He had always picked Father up at the airport on his return from his travels. Many Daughters of Charity were present. The *Hermanitas* of Charles de Foucauld were with them. Silvia and Marta and Father's other helpers knelt close to the casket. Two gray-haired, American-looking ladies could be seen in the crowd. They were Protestant missionaries. And then there were hundreds and hundreds of Otomís, most dressed in the shabby rags they always wore. And these were only the ones who had been informed, who lived close enough to Ixmiquilpan. In the remote villages they did not yet know what had happened.

Bishop Sahagún spoke movingly of Father's love which had given life to an arid desert. Several priests added brief but heartfelt words. The sound of many hundreds of voices joined in song was hauntingly beautiful. Birds flew about within the ancient walls. When the Mass had ended, the throng followed the casket out the main door and down the steps for the long trek to the cemetery. The march took almost an hour, for the cemetery was on the other side of the city. A truck with loudspeakers helped the vast crowd to sing together, to pray the rosary and the litanies. A contingent from Father's favorite village carried a banner reading "J. Villagrán." Groups of four men each took turns carrying the casket on their shoulders. The Protestant plumber who had been Father's next-door neighbor for years relinquished his position only under constraint, tears streaming down his face.

Another Protestant had dug the grave. Father Lino chose for the burial of his dear friend a humble cemetery in the heart of a Protestant *barrio* of the city, hoping and praying that Father's presence there might be a grace to some of the people to return to the faith of their fathers. The coffin was reverently lowered into the grave. Bishop Sahagún gave the final blessing. Then clouds of dust rose into the air as the workers began immediately to fill the excavation with the sandy soil of the Mezquital. Father's priest friends passed the shovel one to another. A balding Mexican priest, hatless in the glaring sun, worked vigorously despite his almost seventy years. Dirt mingled with tears and perspiration to stain his swarthy face. Father Olivieri had been his confessor. Sister Jo placed the final shovelful of earth on her father's grave. It was exactly twenty-four hours since he had drawn his last breath. Then the grave was strewn with bright flowers and the mourners slowly walked away.

Sister Jo was deep in thought. "Ah, Papà," she mused, "you renounced your beautiful home, your family, your place in high society, you even renounced your intellectual life, but you ended by finding everything. Had you remained a great captain, or a great lawyer, or a great professor, you would never have received the homage and the veneration and the devotion manifested today by these simple people as they marched behind you to the cemetery. You have a large family in the United States, an even larger one in Italy, but I am the only one here with any of the old ties. Instead it is the people to whom you gave yourself completely who are with you now."

In the next few days I drove Sister Jo to some of Father's most distant missions so that she could announce the sad news to his friends. We even braved the impossible road to San

Andrés Daboxtha. Many times we returned to his grave. Fresh flowers were there. Rarely was he alone. On one occasion there were over seventy Indians praying the rosary.

Father Alberto Libardoni, O.S.J., who had been his pastor when he was yet a lay catechist, reminisced about his old friend: "From the first it was evident to me that the apostolate of this man was to be the teacher and the servant of the poor. He tried, within his own limits, to follow the injunctions of the Gospel to the fullest, as he saw them. Once I heard a priest say, 'I was born poor, I wish to live among the poor, I wish to work among the poor, and I wish to die poor.' The extraordinary thing about Father Olivieri is that he was not born a poor man, he had not lived as a poor man, he had been a rich man, and yet he found such complete happiness in the life of the poor. It is remarkable to realize that a man so proficient in law, who served military duty with such honor, who associated with people of society, who was revered among the highly cultured as one of their own, should be perfectly satisfied to live among these people by whom he was surrounded. It is easy to talk about leaving your family, leaving your possessions, leaving everything, but it is always done at the cost of a great deal of hardship. It seemed as though these hundreds and hundreds of Indians instinctively realized what a great offering of himself Father Olivieri had made for them. He spoke for them, he spoke about them, he worked for them, he worked with them, he prayed for them, he prayed with them, and he died for them."

"Now that Father Olivieri no longer walks with us in the Valley of the Mezquital," added Father Lino, "people will begin to realize that his life and ministry were a turning point for the overall betterment of the valley. He was a man of deep faith and tremendous patience. Now, I am sure that what we were unable to achieve during his lifetime he will do for us from Heaven. God will listen not only to the prayers of Father Olivieri but to the prayers of the people who will pray to him."

Sister Jo returned to Indianapolis to find hundreds of messages of sympathy from all over the world. Tributes appeared in the newspapers. Countless Masses were offered for the repose of Father's great soul. Donations to charity were made in his name. A Jewish couple planted a tree in Israel in his memory. Monsignor John D. Connolly, Father Richard Beck, O.M.I., and the other priests of Houston who had known Father concelebrated a memorial Mass, attended by many friends, at St. Vincent de Paul Church. Father's family in Rome arranged for a month's mind Mass on April 26 at the Church of San Carlino.

Father Lino sought to erect a simple, artistic chapel for the celebration of Mass over Father Olivieri's grave. At first Sister Jo opposed the idea. She knew that her father wanted only a rough, wooden cross. She relented, however, when Father Lino explained his reasons. Many of the Christianized Otomis still held to their ancient pagan practices regarding their dead. They would bury the body in some deserted place and then take the clothes to the church where they would ask the priest to bless them and then burn them as an act of propitiation for the soul. Father Lino and the bishop felt that if Father Olivieri's grave were made a place of prayer, sooner or later the people would follow their *padrecito* to the hallowed ground.

Bishop Sahagún blessed the *capillita* in October 1973. It was a beautiful, sunny day. Father's loved people were there. Sister Jo and Sister Carlos came from Indianapolis. The bishop told of Father's many honors, titles and accomplishments, all epitomized in and overshadowed by the single word *sacerdote,* priest. Sister Jo has written of Father's final resting place:

The high sweep of wall and roof is of cement—
Father's rugged simplicity.
Does it remind you of the "praying hands"?
The back wall and the floor are of the finest white marble—
his love of refinement and beauty.

The black marble cross tells of our mortality.
The golden one reminds us of our immortality.
No matter the weather, the luminous blue

which is the background for the gold
will always give a radiance.
The black and white marble altar rests over his body.

No doors. No windows.
Father's earthly home while a priest among the Otomi Indians
  was never closed.
In truth, he holds "open house" as they now come to him
  from valley and mountains.
  Children play there.

Father had many titles.
The only one he prized is this one
  written in simple, bold, gold letters:

SACERDOTE HUMBERTO OLIVIERI MANCINI

NACIO EL 12 DE ENERO 1884 EN ITALIA
FALLECIO EL 26 DE MARZO 1973 EN MEXICO